Coping With Difficult Bosses

COPING
WITH
DIFFICULT
BOSSES

BY

Robert M. Bramson, Ph.D.

A Birch Lane Press Book
Published by Carol Publishing Group

A Birch Lane Press Book
Published by Carol Publishing Group
Birch Lane Press is a registered trademark of Carol
    Communications, Inc.
Editorial Offices: 600 Madison Avenue, New York, N.Y. 10022
Sales & Distribution Offices: 120 Enterprise Avenue, Secaucus, N.J.
    07094
In Canada: Canadian Manda Group, P.O. Box 920, Station U,
    Toronto, Ontario M8Z 5P9
Queries regarding rights and permissions should be addressed to
Carol Publishing Group, 600 Madison Avenue, New York, N.Y. 10022

Carol Publishing Group books are available at special discounts
for bulk purchases, for sales promotions, fund raising, or educational purposes. Special editions can be created to specifications.
For details, contact: Special Sales Department, Carol Publishing
Group, 120 Enterprise Avenue, Secaucus, N.J. 07094

Manufactured in the United States of America

10 9 8 7 6 5 4 3 2 1

Library of Congress Cataloging-in-Publication Data

Bramson, Robert M.
    Coping with difficult bosses / by Robert Bramson.
        p.   cm.
    "Birch Lane Press book"
    ISBN 1-55972-139-1
    1. Managing your boss.   2. Interpersonal relations.
3. Organizational behavior.   I. Title.
HF5548.83.B73   1992
650.1′3—dc20   92-17492
                                                   CIP

Contents

Contents

Preface

Ten years ago, convinced that there was indeed a need for such a book, I wrote *Coping With Difficult People*. Its publication changed the nature of my consulting practice. *Coping* brought seemingly endless opportunities to work intensively, with the bosses, and put-upon subordinates of an enormous number of difficult managers and executives. This book is a report on the perspectives, methods, and techniques that proved to be both effective, and do-able, even when the prospects for change seemed initially discouraging, and the leverage the methods provided had to be applied upward into the hierarchy.

Many people contributed to the substance of this book, some knowingly and directly, others more subtly, and often without their knowledge.

My present partners and associates, Susan Bramson, Lucy Gill, Joanne Smyth-Vartanian, and Richard Terrell have provided insight, inspiration, and method. Susan, also my wife, fellow parent, and most candid critic, is a co-developer—along with past partners Allen Harrison and Nicholas Parlette—of the thinking styles framework described in chapter 4. Lucy, also a research associate of the Palo Alto Mental Research Institute, pioneered the application of systemic change techniques to chronic problems in the workplace. Through the years she has particularly enriched my repertoire of effective coping techniques.

Wilson Yandell, my counselor and mentor for many years, and my friend and colleague Walcott Beatty, emeritus professor of psychology at San Francisco State University, have often modeled the importance of a wise and caring sensitivity to both the power and complexities of human interactions.

Richard Lazarus and Alan Monat early on supported the practical value of my "coping" approach, while also pointing out the need for a better enunciated scientific rationale. As a result, I began to study and report on the effects of managerial thinking styles on difficult behavior and sought a broader theoretical basis for the efficacy of coping techniques.

My notions about why and how people in messy interactions often unwittingly promote the continuation of just what they don't want has been richened by the writings of systemic brief therapists, particularly Richard Fisch, John Weakland, Lynn Segal, and Steve de Shazer.

The sections on understanding each of the difficult boss types described in chapters 2 through 6 are my own integration of many interviews with the difficult bosses themselves and the current thinking of both cognitive and dynamic psychologists. Their purpose is to give that "understanding from the inside," to use George Kelly's term, that offers freedom to move beyond fear or indignation, to effective action.

My thanks to my editor Gail Kinn, who aided in the final shaping of the manuscript. Editorial friends Loretta Barrett and Marilyn Abraham, and Carol Mann—my friend and agent for twelve productive years—jointly encouraged me to write this appropriate and needed sequel to my earlier *Coping With Difficult People.*

To Margaret Smith, who turned my marginal scrawls into wonderfully typed manuscripts even unto the fifth revision, and who competently filled in transitions that were unreadable or overlooked, my thanks for being fast, accurate, patient, and always pleasant.

My children Wendy Waits, Marni Welch, Robert Martin Bramson, Sean Gallaher, Patrick Gallaher and Jeremy Bramson have, over the years, kept me honest about my own difficult behavior, an absolute necessity for anyone who professes to help others deal with theirs.

A note on gender usage: Where practicable, I have tried to

avoid the awkward "she or he" or s/he conventions by using the plural form or, alternately, by using he or she when the singular form made more sense. In either case, she is intended to include he, and he to include she, for neither difficult behavior nor the ability to cope with it is the sole province of either sex.

With a few obvious exceptions, the cases and examples found in this book describe real people. The words spoken by the Difficult Bosses and those who coped with them were taken from case notes made shortly after the events occurred and are given only a smidgeon of editorial smoothing. Names, places and, when it would not detract from the value of the example, sex and organizational setting have been changed to conceal the actual identity of both bosses and clients.

Finally, my deepest appreciation to those discouraged, but not defeated, clients who were willing to try a coping approach on their difficult bosses, and to their bosses who then responded by becoming less difficult. Without them, there would be no book.

Coping With Difficult Bosses

1

Introduction: *The Nature of Coping and Why It's a Better Alternative Than Hating, Quitting, or Copping Out*

If you have never been disconcerted, demoralized, or at least mildly depressed by an infuriating, irksome, or inept boss, you are indeed rare. Difficult Bosses demoralize their subordinates, trouble their own superiors, and reduce the productivity potential of the departments they manage. Not all of these frustrating superiors (they are only "superior" in the sense that they're higher ranking, of course) are equally villainous. Some, indeed, have brought such reprehensible behavior patterns to their management jobs that they would qualify as impossible people in any setting. Others, however, are otherwise decent people whose personal liabilities—and we all have them—have been magnified by power and responsibility. But, whether presidents of a mammoth corporation or supervisors of a three-person government office, all Difficult Bosses reduce initiative and innovation, and they frequently start a selective emigration of valuable employees—the best often leave first—to more supportive work environments.

3

Here are two examples of Difficult Bosses who in quite different ways incensed and undermined their victims.

"I'm so furious I can't see straight," said Aggie to her friend. "I asked my boss, Alex, for a raise two months ago, and he assured me he'd recommend it to Tess Wilson, the department head. Now he finally gets around to telling me that she had some questions about whether my job is that much more demanding than the other technicians. Oh, I'm not mad at Wilson—it's her job to keep the lid on salaries. It's that chickenshit Alex. He thinks that Wilson is against anyone getting more money right now and so he isn't doing anything that 'might sound uncooperative.' I always thought bosses were supposed to support their employees and try to get them what they deserve. If he'd tell her that the job I'm doing rates more pay or even just talk to her again, and she still said no, I wouldn't feel so frustrated. But what I'm getting from Alex is nothing!"

"I'll tell you, Mr. Fogel," said Frank Phillips to the division human-resources manager, "I've had my fill of working for Larry Parks. Yesterday afternoon, while I was on the phone with someone in purchasing—trying to mend some fences that Parks knocked over, as a matter of fact—he barged into my cubicle yelling at the top of his lungs. He ordered me not to make any more phone calls without his permission and then accused me of being a disloyal sneak. Now, I might like to see him thrown out on his ear, but I don't go around badmouthing my boss unless I tell him I'm going to do it first, which I did this morning before I came in to see you.

"I've always been pretty easygoing—you know what I mean, not easily upset by other people—but I won't put up with being yelled at, shouted down, and insulted. The fact is, if you can't or won't move me out from under Parks, and right now, I'm quitting. I'll wait for your call." Bernie Fogel watched the door to his office slowly close, sighed, and picked up the hastily scribbled note that Larry Parks had pitched at his desk early that morning. "Fogel," it said, "that young punk Phillips may come in to see you. I know he's one of the fast-track wizards from your management training program, but I will not tolerate anyone countermanding my

orders. If he can't learn who's the boss, I don't want him."
"The feeling's very mutual," said Bernie to no one in particular, "and if you weren't so damn technically brilliant,
Parks, you'd have been out on your ass a long time before
this." Where, Bernie wondered, could he move young Phillips? Even more to the point, where was he going to find
someone who could stick it out with heavy-handed Larry?

For over thirty-five years, first as a worker—both blue-
and white-collar—and then as a consultant to more than
three hundred different organizations, I've worked for,
with, and on Difficult Bosses. Some, like Larry Parks, had
paired a natural flair for hostile intimidation with a high
level of personal competence and parlayed that combination into positions of real power that they misused with
impunity for years. Others, like Alex, were difficult for
precisely the opposite reason. They abdicated the power of
their position, leaving in their wake long-delayed promotions or worthy projects that were aborted too soon because
of insufficient backing. The richness of those consulting
experiences—for the past ten years I have spent almost half
of my consulting time with talented but managerially
flawed executives and their staffs—has left me optimistic
about what can be done when two important realities are
acknowledged: that a Difficult Boss can be a personal disaster, and that you're unlikely to be rescued by anyone else in
your organization.
  The first of these facts may seem obvious if you've suffered at the hands of abrasive, know-it-all, or not-there-
when-you-need-them bosses. What may not be quite so obvious is that they tend to induce in you the most damaging
variety of stress—helpless, angry frustration. Any action
that prevents or minimizes the difficult behavior will help
you feel less helpless.
  The second reality—that you're unlikely to be rescued—
is a particularly bitter pill for those who have loyally supported and served their organizations. But unfair or not,
fellow employees are unlikely to do much to ease your pain,
at least until you have first made some serious efforts at
coping. This is especially so when, despite their trying

behavior, the unsatisfactory supervisors are markedly intelligent or technically able. Because they are respected for their personal accomplishments, they are left alone to work their mischief even when it seems obvious to outside observers that in the long run they are costing the organization more than they are returning to it. Interestingly, many Difficult Bosses do not see themselves as difficult, a tribute to both the awesome power of denial, and the reluctance of *their* superiors to deal directly with them. (To a considerable extent it is the corporation's acceptance of poor people management that makes working for a Difficult Boss so agonizing.) Organizational reluctance to eliminate or at least mitigate ineffective management makes it futile to wish that such bosses would just disappear. They are unlikely to, at least without a little help from you.

Twenty years ago, when I first began to study the behavior of difficult people in work settings, I was struck by how well some people ignored, cheerily put up with, or even worked productively with the same problem persons who had stumped their fellows. Since then, I and my associates have systematically observed and interviewed difficult people, their victims, and those who have learned to handle them. We have noted which coping steps work—and which do not—to nullify or diminish the difficult behavior patterns of hard-to-get-along-with people. Those coping methods, as they apply to the uneasy task of dealing with Difficult Bosses, make up much of the substance of this book.

This book, then, is not a simple tract that lays out in grisly detail how terrible Difficult Bosses can be. Anyone who has suffered under one hardly needs a book to describe what it's like. Rather, it is about how to recognize, understand, and cope with managers like Alex and Larry Parks, and their equally irritating cousins who favor different, but equally debilitating difficult behavior. The practical methods and techniques in each chapter will help you to deal effectively with managers who charge, bully, buffalo, sneak, waffle, or otherwise find their way into your life. The methods have worked successfully for people at every level, in a kaleidoscope of different organizations. Most found that they benefited in several specific ways:

- They felt more in control of their work lives.
- They felt less helpless frustration and anger.
- As their level of emotionality was reduced they were able to think more clearly and objectively about both job and career.
- They reversed the drift into dependency or aggressive incompetence that Difficult Bosses often elicit.
- Their willingness to commit time and energy to their jobs substantially increased.
- They escaped the sense of personal failure that often follows an emotional resignation.

Best of all, as these positive changes began to accrue, the copers valued themselves more and regained a sense of self-worth that had been eroded in the weeks, months, and sometimes years of feeling trapped in an essentially degrading situation. In sum, they felt better, worked better, and, in the process, gained confidence in their ability to productively handle impossible people. You can, too.

What Does "Coping" Mean?

I like the term *coping* because it means "to contend on equal terms"—exactly what one needs to do when dealing with a person who has learned how to take advantage of others through difficult behavior.

While we don't often think about it in that way, all difficult behavior is learned, and in some important ways it provides at least a short-run advantage. For example, almost three-quarters of the employees in the two hundred organizations I and my associates studied over an eleven-year period have reported a "back-pedaling" reaction when under attack by hostile and bullying bosses. When interviewed, blue and white collar alike spoke of feeling confused, even frightened. They usually sat immobilized, looked down at floor, table, or piece of paper, and said nothing. They did, however—albeit with little heart—then carry out whatever orders they had received. To be sure, some of those so attacked reacted in quite the opposite way—with speechless fury at being treated so insultingly. Either way, they were out of commission and the boss was fully in charge. Whether intimidated or emotionally distraught, they did what the boss told them to do, without wasting any of the boss's precious time venturing their own opinions.

The psychological rewards of supervisory bullying are even greater. By demonstrating how weak or out of control *others* are, bosses buttress their own strength and power, a real plus for those who need to quiet their own secret self-doubts.*

Although every difficult behavior pattern is not as concretely rewarding as bullying, each is powerful because it causes others to react in very specific ways. Therefore the basic function of each of the coping techniques you'll find in the pages ahead is to provide you with "substitute" responses—things to do and say other than what you feel like doing or saying. By not responding as your impulses say you should, you break the awful cycle. For example, if you neither cower before bullying nor angrily explode, you will have denied your boss both concrete and psychological payoffs. When difficult behavior no longer "works," most perpetrators will fall back on more reasonable responses than you may have thought them capable of.

Before we move on to examine the how of coping with the disreputable cast of characters that inhabit the following chapters, two further points are worth exploring: a natural reluctance, as a torturee, to "understand" your torturer, and a potential concern that you might be "manipulative."

Why Is It Useful to Understand?

The behavior of managers whose demeanor seems so antithetical to good management is so confounding that most of

---

* Sure, there are long-term costs to abrasive, hostile behavior. Degraded employees are demotivated, afraid to show initiative, and likely to do little more than they have to. But it is the short-term gain that fixes a behavior pattern into the personality (one reason that we all have acquired some habitual responses that we would rather not have).

us are content to simply hate it without trying to make sense of it, or we explain it without much thought as the product of a defective personality. Yet even a modicum of that special kind of understanding that psychologist George Kelly called "understanding from the inside" can help you to stop wishing that your Difficult Bosses were different; this is important because you can only influence others when you see them as they are, not as you wish they were. Seeing people from the inside means formulating, in your own mind, a picture of how the world must look to them, as distorted as that view may seem. In truth, you may not really *want* to understand someone who is behaving badly toward you. If so, it may help you to move beyond that distaste to keep in mind that "understanding" does *not* imply approval, acceptance, or liking, and that understanding from the inside lays a solid foundation for coping. When in later chapters, you find brief descriptions of what it's like to be the very kind of Difficult Boss that you can't abide, expect to feel resistant, but force yourself to read them anyway.

Coping Is Ethical

Coping is always planned and purposeful because it must substitute for natural responses that reward the very behavior you want to stop. At times, you may even find it valuable to write out and rehearse a script before you go into action. For some of you, the notion of behaving without the natural spontaneity that characterizes honest and informal relationships may raise the question, "Isn't it manipulative?" My answer to that question must be yes. Coping effectively *is* manipulative, in the sense that you are not thoughtlessly responding as your feelings urge you to. But for me that is the wrong question. The relevant question is "Is it ethical?" Here, also, I believe the answer is yes. "Coping" is neither a synonym for revenge on obstreperous bosses, nor a euphemism for forgiveness or passive acceptance. You will not be using your bosses' motivations against them. Instead, your goals as a coper will be to find a way of responding to disconcerting behavior that will enable both you, and your frustrating boss, to be as productive as possible in the particular situations in which you find yourselves. For these reasons, I believe that coping is a highly ethical endeavor.

At this point, you may be feeling a bit apprehensive about even thinking of coping with a difficult boss. Take heart; all of the successful copers I've known have faced similar doubts. Your confidence to cope will come from knowing what to do and how to do it safely and honorably—exactly what this book is about.

2

When Your Boss Attacks or Degrades You: *Ogres, Fire-Eaters, and Other Bullying Bosses*

CASE 1 Larry Parks, whom we briefly visited at the beginning of chapter 1, was a technically brilliant engineering manager who was known in the company human-resources office as "Old Grievance Maker." He was sure that his major problems were the "incompetent jerks" in human resources who sent "shitheads and assholes" to work for him. Larry was forty-six years old but looked much younger, a taller, angular man, whose deliberate stride and sardonic expression had earned him another sobriquet—"the gunfighter." Among his less pleasant habits were these: As he stalked through the plant floor, he would suddenly come to an abrupt halt an arm's length from a worker busily typing, assembling, or packaging, and demand, "What are you doing?" He would then wait impatiently for an enlightening response from the cornered individual. It was seldom forthcoming. Shocked into silence, most simply continued, or tried to continue, with their tasks, hoping that he would go away. He would—having once again demonstrated that his world was indeed populated with jerks.

In staff meetings, Larry would break into his subordinates' presentations with such sarcastic gems as—"I must have heard you wrong, Sally, or do you really believe what you just said." He would then insist that Sally answer his "question." Whatever the reply, he would knowingly smirk, inviting his reluctant staff to share his unspoken verdict: "How can anyone be so stupid." When he was chided by the human-resources department for his rough ways, he would smugly point out that he had thoroughly embraced "the management-by-objectives plan that you guys keep telling me will make us all participative managers." Those who worked under him, however, knew that Larry's version of "management by objectives" was "make your numbers, or else." Quarterly progress reviews were miserable affairs in which employees were browbeaten into acknowledging that their performance targets were either too easy if they were met, or, if unmet, yet another example of their laziness or incompetence. When the human-resources manager pointed out that the essence of the corporate management-by-objectives program was employee participation in setting objectives, he was disdainfully faced with an incontrovertible fact—Larry's unit was one of the most productive in the company. In a company that paid both group and individual performance bonuses, those employees who stuck it out with Larry often took home substantial paychecks. Thus the employees with whom I spoke felt whipsawed as much by their own conflicting feelings as by Larry's harassment. As one experienced technician put it, "I have only my greed for those fancy paychecks to blame for not getting out of this hellish place. But that only makes me feel worse."

CASE 2   Picture this: Timothy Ronald, a midwestern state agency director, is meeting with his executive staff at their regular Monday morning planning session. His trim, youthful appearance and pleasant manner don't hint at a sleepless Sunday night spent reliving two thorny hours in which the irate state governor had berated Tim for making "politically dangerous" statements at a recent press conference. Nonetheless, Tim was a thorough professional and he moved smoothly through the Monday meeting agenda, until the discussion turned to a change in agency policy that the governor had "hoped might be made." Hal, one of Tim's deputies, snorted at the potential change and quipped, "Well, I hope you told the guv off about that dumb idea."

"Do you have any doubt about who's running this department," gritted out Tim, his teeth clenched, his face red. "When I want any stupid remarks from you, I'll ask for them. Until then, sit back, shut up and just listen, and that goes for everyone else in this room!"

Hal sat there frozen, his eyes flickering from side to side, to see how the other deputies were taking it. He found little comfort. Some stared at the table; some, red-faced and embarrassed, tried to smile as if it were an extension of Hal's joke; all wished themselves somewhere else.

There are many ways bosses can overwhelm, intimidate, and generally run over those who work for them, but Larry Parks and Tim Ronald exemplify the two most complained about. I call their kind respectively Ogres and Fire Eaters, because their power comes largely from a neat capacity to overwhelm by evoking buried childhood fears. In many ways they are alike. Both openly attack, often with little provocation, driving their victims into silent confusion or speechless rage. Yet they are different enough to make it worthwhile to take them up separately.

Later in the chapter we will return to the task of understanding and coping with Fire Eaters, and the fate of Tim's miserable group. But let's start with those most formidable of intimidators, the Ogres.

Recognizing Ogres

Ogres like Larry Parks often provoke groans from concerned human-resources mangers, and almost as frequently they elicit smiles—albeit concealed from their human-resource colleagues—from the senior executives who only measure bottom-line results. Therefore, complaints to higher management often generate only an embarrassed silence and little direct action. Sometimes there may be little "suggestions" to Larry that he "improve his communication style." More often, however, Ogres' bosses shy away from doing *anything* that might disturb those golden production figures. But such a laissez-faire attitude on the part of senior management flies in the face of several realities. For one thing, high production and a considerate attitude are not mutually exclusive. It is possible to be demanding and still treat employees with respect. Although Ogres can bully employees into doing what they're told, and thus force high performance in routine activities, there are long-term losses, both to the organization and to the Ogre's own promotability. Discouraged, frightened, angry workers are seldom creative or committed to anything but resistance, while today's complex problems and fast-moving environments need enthusiasm and lively minds, not grudging automatons.

To be fair, not all intimidating bosses are as obviously Ogre-ish as Larry Parks. Some are more subtle in their sarcasm and most treat their superiors and colleagues with respect, if not admiration. With staff members or colleagues who demonstrate the same strengths they value in themselves, Ogres often develop a rough camaraderie.

Understanding Ogres

Three personal factors meld to produce intimidating bosses: a thinking process that is attuned to rapid and confident decision making, a need to feel powerful and influential, and a hidden—at least from themselves—vein of self-doubt.

Quick, Confident Thinking People who are quick to make up their minds are a pleasure to work with when fast, confident action is the ticket. In ten years of studying managerial thinking styles, my associates and I have found that people with minds like these—we call them Realist thinkers—bring many positive qualities to any situation.

They cut through subtleties and extraneous data to the core of a problem, and they move straight on to fix whatever is broken. Sure, they may be satisfied with less than the best solution, they may act before all of the facts are in and get unreasonably irritated when others hesitate because they want more data, or because they think the plan hasn't been adequately checked out with other players. Certainly, all Realist thinkers are not Ogres (although they may look that way to those of us who are more attuned to considered decisions or who believe in consulting others). It is when Realist thinkers also have a strong need to be in control that they can become overpowering.

A Need for Power   We all want and need similar things, but we do not want them to the same degree. For example, some of us need prestige and visibility to feel content, but for others standing out in the crowd holds little interest. The latter may, however, relish the approval of friends and coworkers. Still others care little about acceptance or attention, but can't rest easy without the power to influence. It's in this group that we find the Ogres of the world. They are driven by an insistent inner push to strive for the top of any pecking order, and they feel depressed when they are forced to take a backseat.*

Yet that is only two-thirds of the picture. While rapid-fire thinkers with a strong drive for control are always hard to ignore, the harsh, intimidating aspect of Ogres stems largely from a third inner ingredient—an unremitting need to validate themselves, to prove that they are indeed worthy.

The Need for Self-Validation   Ogres desperately need to assure themselves of their strength and importance by demonstrating your weakness and lack of consequence. Whether you back down or explode in anger, they demonstrate to

---

* Studies of identical twins, who share the same genetic inheritance, seem to demonstrate that much of one's motivation repertoire is inherited. If so, dominating people did not choose to have a need for power, they were saddled with it.

you, and more vitally, to themselves, just how superior to you they are.

Not unexpectedly, Ogres value strength in others, *if* they don't feel personally challenged by it. In my private conversations with them, I have become accustomed to scathing complaints about "yes" people who never argue with their decisions. A curious objection from the same worthies who readily crush anyone daring to voice an opposite opinion. Yet it is this paradoxical perspective of Ogres that best explains why the coping methods outlined in the next section work so well. Although Ogres are often disparagingly labeled "basically insecure," as indeed they are, they are seldom aware of this flaw and vociferously deny it. To the contrary, they feel confident, powerful, and impatient with those whom they see as truly the weak ones. True, there are longer-term costs to pushing people around; however, long-term effects do not fix behavioral characteristics into one's personality, but short-term satisfactions, if they are profound enough, do. Unfortunately, beating up on people who deserve it because they're weak—especially if the bully is not overly endowed with sensitivity to others' hurts—is enormously self-reinforcing. Equally unfortunate, some organizations support such behavior. They glorify the "leader" who gets more work out of people than they might otherwise wish to provide and—public speeches to the contrary—they seem willing to accept longer-term costs.

In your own Ogre watching, keep in mind that this mix of inner forces will differ from one individual to another. For example, quick-thinking Realist thinkers pushed by a strong need for power but also blessed with at least a modicum of self-worth are often content to simply be the dominating member of a group without having to make much noise about it. Coping with them may require little more than letting them know that you know that they are in charge. In contrast, the more bosses are driven by worries about being incurably unlovable, the greater will be a need to advertise to others what powerful people they are. So, when your intimidating boss brags about "running the whole show," you may have to work harder and persist longer in your coping efforts.

How to Cope With Ogres: What to Avoid

The magic of Ogre-ing is that it provokes just those responses that make it work—silent acquiescence, righteous complaining, appeasement, or angry rebellion. Each of these reactions is a natural defense against attack. However, there are good reasons to try to control these very human reactions as much as possible. Let's take them one at a time.

Silent Acquiescence John Franks was one of Larry Park's most competent subordinates. He was by nature a quiet, low-key person, who found Larry's behavior impossible to understand and especially reprehensible from someone of Larry's rank. John reacted to Larry with silent, stiff immobility. When the sandblasting or sermon—whichever was his portion for the day—was over, he would, without comment, dutifully proceed to do what he could to carry out Larry's orders. To John, silence and withdrawal were the only rational responses left to him. After all, he said, complaining, or arguing in public, were unprofessional. Larry was puzzled by John. He recognized John's ability and had even remarked to me that he always completed his assignments well and on time. (When I asked Larry whether he had ever mentioned this to John, he said, with a smirk, "Well now, Bob, we don't want to spoil the troops, do we?") He was surprised that John was a "yes" person who would not stand up for himself. (Larry, by the way, was emphatic about the importance of treating everyone equally and behaved accordingly. He bashed everyone even-handedly, without regard for race, creed, or ethnic origin, and to be fair, gave important promotions to female members of his staff.) To Larry, however, John's behavior meant abject surrender, a stance he neither understood nor respected.

Righteous Complaining It's not surprising that Ogres are repeatedly complained about and at times even complained at. Complaining is what most of us do when we believe that something is wrong, but we feel powerless to change it. However, complaining at or about an intimidating boss has two strikes against it. The whining, passive tone that always accompanies complaining is—to some extent realistically—taken as a sign of weakness, thus provoking even sharper attacks. Further, while "Why do you always have to yell at me?" does express a grievance, it also accuses. An Ogre's defensive response to an accusation is always another attack.

How about complaining about a terrible boss to peers, friends, or family members? Doesn't telling a sad story to others provide at least the illusion of control over a bad situation? Isn't complaining a useful vehicle for venting feelings that might otherwise accumulate and cause a stress overload? Yes, in part. In balance, however, the negatives outweigh the positives. For one thing, hearing yourself recite a litany of complaints can not only add stress but may even exaggerate the magnitude of the problem. Psychologist Carol Tavris has pointed out that a lengthy expression of anger may intensify rather than dilute it.

Worse, friends or family, in their well-meaning efforts to sympathize, can make it difficult for you to give up the role of helpless victim. While complaining is a most understandable response to feeling put upon, it can interfere with taking steps that might minimize the behavior you dislike.

Appeasement   Some people have found it worthwhile to learn how to fit in, whatever the situation. Rather than resist, they try to placate their enemies with friendliness and service. Unfortunately, while "I've made fresh coffee," and "I worked late so you'd have the report," can often be the ticket to a ripple-free life, they will be seen by Ogres as still another sign of that softness which invites further humiliation and attack. Larry Parks's secretary, whom he had inherited from his predecessor, was a diligent fifty-three-year-old European-born woman, who tried hard to please him. He privately referred to her as "Ms. Goody," and was impatient with her continual efforts to be helpful, wishing that she would once in a while raise her voice, just to show "that there was a real human being there." Nonetheless, her efforts to please him, and her secretarial skills, did save her from the worst of his tirades. From that standpoint, appeasement may be a workable last resort when other coping efforts have failed. However, like complaining and silent acquiescence, such accommodation does little to reduce the Ogre's demeaning attitude. Over time, the result can be a continued depletion of your own store of self-esteem and a more and more passive stance.

Rebellion Most of us can eventually be provoked to fight, and Ogres are skilled at providing that provocation. Who has not gleefully fantasized cutting down a snide, abusive boss with a few delicious sarcasms of her own. Tempting as this scenario is, there are some excellent reasons to avoid it.

First of all, you're likely to lose the fight. Most Ogres started their battling careers early in life, and have had ample opportunity to hone their skills. You, on the other hand, are an amateur. You lack the years of practice in insult, simulated rage, and other basic maneuvers of verbal in-fighting that are part of any accomplished Ogre's armament. Worse, you are a well-bred, civilized person who understands that brawling should be relegated to alleyways, if even there. You are laden with inhibitions that firmly tell you that problems are best resolved by reasonable discourse, not loud voices. How can you match vituperation with a master, if, in the midst of battle, you find yourself thinking, there must be a better way to handle this than yelling in the hallway. Ogres, on the other hand, are seldom bothered by such inhibitions. Further, they will be driven by their need for self-validation to escalate the fight and to move to levels of personal insult that you will regret.

Then there is the obvious danger that you might, indeed, outpoint your boss and leave him defeated and demoralized. If the person you have squelched is also the one with power to reward, punish, and promote, your satisfaction is likely to be short lived.

Contending with the paradox of a boss who is contemptuous if you show weakness but pulverizes you when you fight back, is the main thrust of the coping methods that follow.

How to Cope With Ogres: What to Do

The essence of coping with Ogres is to simultaneously show that while you have your own source of strength, you are not a threat to the Ogre's own need to feel strong and competent. The rub is that you must do all that just when your inner voices are urging you to faint, fight, or fall back. There are certainly times when honest spontaneity is the key to improved human relationships, but while you are being harpooned by a hostile boss is not one of those times. It is then that you need to do what actors do—communicate emotions you do not feel. Start by controlling those elements of your body posture that are relatively easily managed: hold yourself erect, don't back away, and look your intimidator in the eye (or thereabouts).

Watch Your Posture   Picture yourself under attack by a bullying boss well equipped with glaring eyes, flaring nostrils, red face, and grim expression. Before you are even aware it's happening, if you're like most of those I've interviewed, your initial reaction would have been to slump submissively—shoulders rounded, eyes turned down— edging slowly away from your attacker. Now, however, your newfound coping skills come to your rescue. You straighten up, turn to face the Ogre and, willing yourself to do it, steadily look into its eyes. Does your tormentor magically melt? Unfortunately, no. Yet you've made progress because you will have signaled that you are somebody of substance, neither retreating nor getting ready to fight. Do you find those "death-ray beams," as one client named them, that emanate from your boss's eyes are too intense? If so, you can gaze at the nose, the forehead, the point of the chin. Your boss won't know the difference and it will have almost the same effect.

   I think you'll also find that speaking up, that is, projecting your voice loudly enough to be easily heard, will come more naturally when you are looking at the person to whom you are speaking. Having shown your substance by standing erect and speaking up, you're ready to move on to the next step—calling your boss by name.

Humanize the Relationship   Most people, Ogres included, get a lift when they hear their names. Even more important, I believe that naming people humanizes the relationship a bit. It's easier for bosses to stomp on people after they have put an alien stamp on them and thus taken away their humanity. It's much easier to derogate "slobs," "loafers," or "punks" than "Sallys," "Sams," or "Marys." Therefore, try to start your conversations with a hostile boss by calling her by name (even though calling her *a* name might reflect your true feeling). Keep consistent with your usual form of address; don't switch to "Mrs. Smith" when you've been on a first-name basis with Rhonda, nor switch to "Rhonda" when she's been generally known to you as Mrs. Smith. Such name switches are often used to put others in their place—"Rhonda May Smith, where were you last night?"—and are thus provocative, rather than humanizing.

Similarly, when the occasion makes it appropriate, over coffee, say, bring up interesting aspects of your life. A few stories about past adventures or family happenings may break or at least bend the stereotype that's found its way into your boss's mind. The point you want to convey is that you're not just a silly secretary, dull engineer, or wimpy accountant, you're a person who's meeting the challenges of a unique life.

Don't Argue, Disagree   To a hostile-aggressive person, "You're wrong" or "That's not true" are fighting words, more likely to provoke a counterattack than careful attention to your points. Instead, memorize a few responses that do not directly contradict, yet open the way for you to present your own views strongly. Such expressions such as "In my judgment. . . ." or "In my opinion. . . ." will keep you in the conversation without directly contending that your boss is incorrect. The best of these self-referent statements is "I disagree," especially if it is followed with a request for more enlightenment. For example, "Tom, I think maybe I disagree with you, but tell me more about what's on your mind." Much of the power of these responses is that they undo the stereotype that Tom has of you. You are not weakly compliant, nor resistant or argumentative. Instead, you are calmly (well, as calmly as possible, anyway) asking him to tell you more.

Break the Spell   It is often helpful to interrupt the flow of whatever is happening. Rise from your chair if you are seated, walk over to a desk, lean against it, or sit on the edge of it, bend to pick up a pencil that you might even have purposefully dropped. Your aim will be to produce a brief natural break in the interaction. Those few seconds can help you to think through the next steps in your coping strategy, and may even help the Ogre to become aware that this interplay is somehow different from most others.

Capitalize on Interruptions   Realist thinkers are great interrupters. They see it as a kind of efficiency of mind. Having heard the first few sentences of your paragraph, they are certain that they can anticipate the rest. It's simply good sense for them to interrupt, thereby saving time. Even better, by cutting you off, especially with remarks such as "I've already heard that," they demonstrate that they have both the right and the power to do so. You can turn this to your advantage by interjecting "Tom, you interrupted me," as calmly as you can. (Smiling when you say it doesn't seem to detract from its effectiveness.) "You interrupted me," a simple statement of a fact, doesn't carry the same emotional baggage as "Don't interrupt me"—fighting words—or "Please don't interrupt me," a weak appeal. Either is likely to provoke Tom to show you that he certainly can interrupt you. Having called Tom on the interruption, continue with the points you were making, doing your best to stay unhurried and matter-of-fact. Emphasize facts or alternate actions to be taken rather than what is wrong with your boss's idea. Be ready to be interrupted again—most Ogres are hard players—and just as ready to break back in with "Tom, you interrupted me." (Watch out for the provocative: "You interrupted me, *again*.") This coping technique has two benefits. First, you have defined yourself as a substantial person, but in a way that does not wrest control from its rightful possessor. Second, you have focused attention on the problems to be solved rather than the personalities involved. You'll know that you have gained ground if your boss responds by: staring at you as if he has never seen you before; looking puzzled; listening, albeit impatiently, to your comments about the problem; and, at length, joining in a discussion about the most appropriate action to take. Most aggressive bosses are truly interested in correcting things that have gone wrong, although this is often obscured by their fierceness. In addition to their skill in running over others, it is this "corrective thinking" quality that moves them so far up in many organizational hierarchies. Again, back to the fundamental precept of this book: When Ogres' difficult behavior doesn't have its expected effect, when it doesn't reduce you to silence, tears, or impotent rage, even such bad actors as these will usually show a more productive side.

When You Can't Talk, Write   Many intimidators have discovered that a deliciously abusive way to display their superiority is to verbally put others in their place, and then cut them off by walking away, switching off the fax, or hanging up the phone. If you are ever blocked by that neat, if nasty, move, never trail after your nemesis hoping somehow to have your say. Certainly it is vital that you do something to maintain your sturdy-but-non-threatening image. But there is a great chance that in your turbulent state you may not maintain your composure. Instead, respond with an informal note—not a formal memorandum or letter—in which you make the points that were lost when you were abruptly cut off. It might look something like this: "Barbara, yesterday we didn't fully discuss the second of the two recommendations that I made in the price-increase proposal. Although I'm not quite sure what you had in mind, I believe that the proposal covers many of the things you were worried about. I'd like to meet tomorrow morning and iron out the details of my next step. If I don't hear to the contrary, I'll see you in your office at 8:30." If possible, show your note to a coworker, friend, or family member, for a check that a whining tone has not found its way into what should have been a matter-of-fact statement. Then, drop it off, mail it, or fax it.

Keep Them Posted   Angry confrontations with an Ogre can often be prevented by a timely notification of potential problems. Your purpose is to prevent the Ogre from finding out from a third party that something might be awry. As soon as you can, inform the Ogre of the problem, pointing out that you have a plan for regaining control. Resist, however, asking his or her advice, since having asked for help from aggressive quick thinkers you're likely to get it. Under pressure to accept their ideas, stupid or not, or to argue against them, you may end up with an unworkable plan or a confrontation you don't need. If your simple statement that you have a plan is questioned, be ready to briefly outline what you intend to do. Accept your boss's comments as input that you gratefully acknowledge by replying, "Good thoughts, Barbara, I'll try to work them into my plan and, of course, I'll keep you posted."

Acknowledge the Ogre's Strength and Competence   As in the example just given, you can strengthen your position vis-a-vis hard-headed bosses by commenting frequently on either the merit of points they have made, or their general competence. Such phrases as "I think that your last point is on the money," or "You're usually up to date on these things, Tom," will help them listen to your own notions of what needs to be done, especially if you take pains to avoid preceding your expressions with "But," since most people automatically assume a defensive posture when they hear "That's very true, but. . . ." Experience has taught them that they will then be shown why their ideas are not very true at all. A better form is "And, here are a few more thoughts for the action plan." What if you do indeed see flaws in the boss's proposal? My suggestion is to try to make whatever corrections are necessary, by proposing modifications or additions to the tactics or strategy proposed, not by refuting the logic behind your boss's thoughts. For example, you might believe your boss's plan seems too precipitous, and that a delay, or a more step-by-step approach, would work better. As an alternative to "We're moving too fast"—a direct challenge—try "And, it might even work better if we stretched out our marketing thrust over three months so the others won't feel that we are railroading it through."

Prepare a Fall-back Position   It is possible that your first attempts at coping with a boss of Larry Park's ilk may not go smoothly. Perhaps your "I think I disagree" provokes an angry tongue lashing. Or, because you falter in the execution of another coping technique, you are tersely dismissed. In those moments, you are likely to feel nonplussed, discouraged, and even on the verge of acquiescent silence, tears, or an angry explosion. You can forestall the worst situation by using what you know about Ogres to sketch out a fall-back position in case your coping attempts go awry. If they do, the odds are that somehow you have unintentionally nettled your intimidator's deep-seated concerns about self-worth or loss of control. Therefore, a loud and pointed clarification that your intention was not to challenge anyone's status or authority should repair the rift. You might say it something like this: "Wait a minute, Larry, it sounds as if you think that I don't know you're the boss. That's not the case, and whatever you decide on, I will do." If you have caught your boss's attention, follow it up with your version of: "Just like you, I want to make sure that we do our job as well as possible." Whether or not this approach defuses your boss, at least you will have done something other than cower or counterattack, the assuredly natural, but just as assuredly ineffective, responses that set the stage for future assaults.

Coping With Ogres in Action   Janet Price was one person who had learned how to deal with Larry Parks. She was head of his design section, and one of the few staff members he liked. As Larry put it, she "produces a lot, generally does what she's told, and is willing to set me straight when I get off base." I soon had an opportunity to see for myself what he meant.

The general manager of Larry's division had mandated that he work with me to improve his "interpersonal skills" (although Larry was clearly of the opinion that it was the incompetence of most of his staff rather than his own managerial abilities that needed fixing). Recognizing the inevitability of having to appear cooperative, Larry invited me to sit in on a forthcoming staff meeting. He just might, he said, "pick up some pointers on how to make nice." About twenty-five minutes into the meeting, Larry began to outline a new procedure to be followed in working with the corporate purchasing office, which he felt had been usurping his authority as a line manager by mistakenly sacrificing quality for a lower price. His eyes moved from person to person as he made his points, the heel of his hand thumping the table to show he meant business. "I want every one of you (*thump*) to make sure that all (*thump*) of your purchase requests have detailed specifications (*thump, thump*). I don't trust those assholes' common sense one inch (*thump*), and I don't want any (*thump*) one (*thump*) of you jokers to take the easy way out of a little work."

At that point, Janet broke in. "Wait a minute, Larry, are you saying that I might not carry out your orders? Say more about that."

Taken a little aback, Larry said, "I just don't want those guys to think they can push us around."

"I don't either," said Janet, "and I have some thoughts about how to make your plan work better; do you want to hear them now, or should I send you a note?"

"I'm always interested in improvements," said Larry. "A note will be just fine."

During subsequent interviews with other members of Larry's staff, I mentioned this interchange as an example of an effective way to fence in some of Larry's insulting behavior. Two of them admitted that they had seen Janet face up to Larry on several other occasions, but they were certain that if they tried the result would be disaster. Within six months, the same two had discovered that they were wrong. What Janet had done was not magic. She had learned to respond to the anger she felt at Larry's bullying ways with a few techniques that usually worked, but, even if they hadn't, left her no worse off.

Thus far in this chapter, we've considered those tyrannical bosses who harshly, and with intention, overwhelm your ability to function well. Next in line are their close cousins, a highly emotional and out-of-control species for whom the name Fire Eaters seems most apt.

The Fire Eaters

While Fire Eaters combusting into action may resemble their Ogre-ish relatives, there are enough differences in tone and intention to enable you to tell one from the other.

The Behavior of Fire Eaters *Irritable, moody, hot-tempered,* and *explosive* are terms that I frequently hear applied to Fire Eaters. Those who work for them, seeing their bosses switch from reasonable to rabid with disconcerting rapidity, often characterize the experience as life on the lip of a volcano, never sure of how or when the next emotional eruption will burst forth. I've worked with more than a few people who, while sturdy enough to stomach the meanness of intimidating Ogres, are shaken by the sudden rages of a Fire Eater, especially when a few moments before, he or she had been engaged in calm discussion. Office administrator Rhoda Walsh described the managing partner of the medical group for whom she worked this way:

> Most of the time, Dr. Miller is pretty easy to get along with. He's a little set in his ways about procedures, and in the morning he sometimes comes in a little sour, but we've all learned to live with that—you know, stay out of his way until he gets over it. But sometimes—and it's often not about something vital—he will suddenly lose his temper, let go a few sharp remarks, and then begin pounding the table and screaming at us. I'm sometimes so shocked that I can't say a word. I usually just sit there and wait for it to blow over. It's really kind of weird in a way, because later he'll come back

to my desk and apologize. Of course, that doesn't help much, in fact it even makes it a little worse because I know that he wants me to tell him that it's all right when that's not the way I feel at all. Dr. Miller is a nice man and a good doctor, but I'm not sure how long I can keep working in a place where I'm never sure when the fur is going to fly.

If they are aware of the pain they cause, some Fire Eaters, like Dr. Miller, show remorse after their outbursts. Most, however, are oblivious to the full effect they have on others. Take, for example, the Fire-Eating director who punctuated his angry outbursts by printing in bright red ink on whatever report, memo, or letter that infuriated him: "This is stupid," and then sent it down through channels to its originator. When I confronted him with the disastrous effect this was having on staff morale, he was at first incredulous. He could not believe that everyone did not understand that "I think they are wonderful people, I just lose my temper now and then, but they know I really don't mean it."

Understanding Fire Eaters   Fire Eaters' sudden and often seemingly unprovoked outbursts are the product of two simultaneous inner events: feeling personally threatened while, at the same time, under pressure to take some sort of action. To better understand why such mostly sensible people suddenly turn into unreasonable screamers, let's briefly examine what it means to say that someone feels "personally threatened."

We all know what it means to be threatened with a knife or a gun; we fear for our lives or harm to our bodies. What *personally threatens* us is a fear that we will be deprived of what we want the most, to be liked and approved of, to have our achievements recognized, or to be seen by those we respect as competent and in charge. The "threats" involved often seem inconsequential to casual observers: an apathetic reaction to a clever idea, a luncheon party to which one has not been invited, intricate questions asked of a panicky boss with a desparate need to do something, anything. Even when unintended, the resulting hurts can still feel like a punch in the vitals. After such blows to our self-esteem, most of us, like hurt animals, tend to search for privacy, even if it's only the privacy of our own minds. We figuratively lick our psychic wounds and then jump back into the fray. Frequently, however, there is no time for comforting ourselves; we are pressed, right *now*, to decide, to do something. It is in these pressured situations that we dredge up the deeply implanted defensive strategies that helped us as two-year-olds when we felt frustrated, angry, or fearful. Examples of these timeless tactics are foot-stamping tantrums, heartrending sobs, super-cute smiles, sullen pouts, and silent acquiescence. In later years, of course, these primitive responses are clothed in "adult talk"—verbal blows substitute for the windmilling fists of childhood—but their object is the same: to extricate us from an untenable situation or to help get something that we desperately want.

Like the childhood tantrums they resemble, the sudden furies of Fire Eaters seem almost uncontrollable, and in a sense they are. From the perspective of a Fire Eater like Dr. Miller, his abrupt fits of anger happen to him as unpremeditatedly as they happen to you. Understanding why the sudden storms arise may help you feel less irritated by a shamefaced apology from someone who blasted you an hour ago. It may also help you to see that Fire Eaters, as hurtful as they can sometimes be, are more in need of help than of censure.

Coping With Fire Eaters

Doing anything sensible when you've just been bombarded by a Fire-Eating Boss is not easy. So any coping steps must be simple, straightforward, and effective, even if you fumble a bit when carrying them out. These four moves generally satisfy all of those requirements: wait until the boss runs down, get his or her attention, say something to repair the threat and prevent recycling, and temporarily break off the interaction.

Let the Fire Eater Run Down   Fire Eaters usually run out of steam. As the red mist clears, they start to realize that, responsible and civilized as they may otherwise be, they have raged at you, a trusty staff member. They are nonplussed, often shamed into paralyzed silence, and—at least if the ability hasn't been pounded out of them as children— may shed a few tears. Waiting for them to run down saves the effort of forcing your way into the interaction.

Get His or Her Attention   At times, however, the angry outburst won't ease off and you must interrupt the Fire Eater, or get his attention in other ways. Neutral statements like "Wait a minute!" "Stop!" "Yes!" or simply repeating the person's name, loudly and sharply, will often break through.

There are two important reasons for breaking in. First, it's vital that you rapidly proceed to the next coping step, repairing the threat that got the Fire Eater going. Second, it's wise to prevent your Fire Eater from saying things that can't be taken back. A Fire Easter's tirade can escalate to unkind, even brutal, personal remarks, the memory of which may last and never be completely erased.*

Repair the Threat   As soon as possible after the yelling slows or stops, you must repair the threat that set the whole thing off in the first place. Sometimes you may be all too aware of what threatened your boss. For example, you may suddenly realize that while selling your boss on a new procedure you had inadvertently implied that the old procedure—her procedure—was stupid. More often, however, you may not have an inkling of what went wrong. In either case, you must, through words, voice, and attitude, urgently convey the urgent message that you take your boss seriously, that you are interested in what she has to say, and that your intention is to be supportive. Use words such as

---

* In work settings, where you will encounter Fire-Eating Bosses, attacks are always verbal. However, Fire Eaters encountered out of the work setting can, in fact, leave others maimed or dead, as your daily paper will regularly attest. In case you meet up with one of these, carry through with these coping steps, but make sure of your physical safety, for instance, by keeping a barrier between you and the Fire Eater, or keeping your distance while making your coping statements.

"Just a minute, Boss, this sounds really important. Can you say again what you mean," "I know you know a lot about these things; what do you want us to do," or "You know, I really value your opinion a lot, let's go back and start at the beginning." Starting your phrases with the word *Boss* or *Chief*, or whatever rank designation is usual for you (if you seldom or never use anything but your boss's name, *don't* change it now) can in itself have a threat-easing effect if status or power are important.

Easing the threat will help to prevent a particularly distressing sequel to a Fire Eater attack—a recycled explosion just when things seemed to be calming down. You may have been nonplussed by just such an off-setting aftermath as part of an emotional "discussion" at home. First, there is an outburst which, after a time, burns itself out. Relieved, you think to yourself, now we can get at this problem sensibly, and embark in a quiet, reasonable way to get at the facts, only to find your Fire Easter exploding anew. Of course you didn't intend it, but still, it is likely that you had a part in creating this continuing show of fireworks. The Fire Eater, ordinarily a civilized, caring person, having abruptly come to full awareness that he has just screeched at a fellow human being, feels embarrassed, ashamed, and angry with himself—in other words, personally threatened. The social pressure to say something was all that was needed to elicit another furious attack. Your part in this continuing debacle was not letting him know that you indeed take him seriously. Two other coping steps will help to interrupt this painful recycling sequence: temporarily breaking off the interaction and moving to privacy.

Break Off the Interaction   When everyone involved is showing signs of emotional overload, confusion, fear, or anger, almost anything can provoke a resurgence of defensive behavior. So, any excuse for a breather can help. Some possibilities, all of which I've seen work, are: "Excuse me, but I've just gotta hit the john," "I've got to return a phone call," and "I need a few minutes to think over what's been said." Just raising your hand palm out (the familiar "stop" gesture) and then—head bowed showing deep concentra-

tion—writing notes about the *content* of the orders you had
screamed at you (well censored, of course) can work. Whatever reason you give for interrupting the excitement, it's
vital that you tell all concerned just when you intend to get
back in touch. Equally important, hold to that time commitment. For example, if, after a confrontation, you manage a
"Wait a minute, I need a little time to think; I say we break
now for ten minutes," don't let anything—a conference
with a fellow worker, a phone call from a family member—
delay your return to the meeting. A late return may further
put off your Fire Eater and you will have lost the advantage
that the break might have provided.

Make It Private Almost as important as the break is
enabling the Fire Eater to be alone for a short time. Privacy
can prevent a momentary irritation from escalating into a
full-blown battle. If complete privacy is impossible, try to
reduce the number of witnesses to your boss's loss of control. Suggest that the two of you go into a nearby office or
conference room.

Identify the Mood Cycle, if Possible

Some people are "moody" by nature. They tend to cycle
between feeling somewhat better and somewhat worse over
a period that may range from weeks to months. That doesn't
mean that they won't feel boosted by good news, or regretful
of bad during both cycles, but when they're blue they are
more likely to feel disheartened by mildly negative events
and not elated by the truly positive, and, of course, the
opposite is true. During their "up" cycles, they will tend to
overlook, or take with equanimity, all but the most cata-
strophic happenings and to find immense satisfaction in
even moderate upswings. Miles Harder, human-resources
vice president for a large corporation, put it this way, when
talking about his boss:

> Frank is just a moody guy. Right now, all of the things I've
> ever complained about—angry outbursts at meetings, micro-

managing people who are fully capable of running their own shows—are almost nonexistent. If I didn't know better, I'd think he had turned over a new leaf. But I know that sometime, maybe two months from now, his mood is going to swing the other way, and even trivial things will set him off. While it hasn't changed his behavior, understanding these cycles has made my life easier. When he's down, I do everything I know to avoid confrontations. When he's up, I can relax a little and not worry about how well I'm sticking to my coping plan.

Identify Your Boss's Sensitivities The more you can discern the likely causes of your boss's explosions, the better your chances of heading them off. Your list might include situations similar to these actual triggering events:

- Missed deadlines about which the boss wasn't prewarned.
- Staff members coming late to meetings (even though the meetings were boring and poorly run).
- Phone calls to the boss from husband, wife, friend.
- Typos or misspelled names.
- Production or cost-accounting reports that made a department—and consequently the boss—look bad.

Whether or not anyone should *ever* lose control over such ordinary occurrences is beside the point. What *is* useful is taking preventive pains: avoiding typos, holding off pressing or difficult decisions until you see how your boss reacts to that phone call from home.

How About Direct Confrontation? Is there any point in confronting Fire Eaters with the negative effects of their attacks? There are several reasons to think so. First, Fire Eaters are often ignorant of the full consequences of their behavior. They have rarely, consciously and explicitly, chosen to render their staff members irate, indisposed, or impotent. Second, while many of them might not be able to prevent their angry outbursts, there is much they can do to lessen their size and severity. Third, you may feel less trapped if you've had a chance to openly bring out how their difficult behavior is affecting you.

To avoid having your attempt at honesty trigger yet another explosion, you'll need to think through what you plan to say and how you plan to say it. Writing a script is often a good idea, doing your best to eliminate any hint of accusing, nagging, or complaining. The basic format is "When this happens, I react in this way, and that has these effects." In chapter 7, in the section on "behavior blindness," you'll find some specific suggestions for making this a productive and relieving conversation.

Coping With Fire Eaters in Action

Let's now return to the point at which we had cut the action in the second case that opened this chapter—the silence that followed Tim Ronald's angry slash at his deputy, Hal. Actually, the silence lasted at most ten seconds, but at the time it seemed like ten hours. It was Diana, Tim's chief deputy, who finally moved in.

"Tim, whatever the governor asked you to do is always important. We're with you one-hundred percent. Uhhh, how about taking ten right now? We'll come back and talk about where we go from here. I've got something I need to go over with you, myself, so let's meet in your office for a few minutes. That okay?"

With that said, Diana stood up and waited.

"Yeah, I guess so," Tim finally got out. He was staring down at the table, rubbing his hand back and forth on the edge just in front of him.

Diana broke the tension: "Everybody back here in half an hour."

When Diana started for the door, I caught up with her in the hallway to commend her for doing a good job with the coping steps that she and I had discussed, and rehearsed, the week before.

She said, "I'm glad you thought it was okay—I was certainly the opposite of calm and collected when I was doing it. I couldn't think of what to say. You were right, though,

Tim took it and he seems back on a reasonable track. Right now, I've got to think of something to talk to him about when I meet with him in five minutes. The main thing I was trying for was to get him away from the rest of the guys. He's not the only one who needs to pull himself together."

Humor and Hostile-Aggressiveness

Both Ogres and Fire Eaters can be disarmed by humor. However—and it's a major however—it must be the right sort of humor, a comment, said without malice, that delivers two equally emphasized messages: 1) "I recognize and appreciate your strength," and 2) "But I'm not blown away by it." The following examples illustrate how two people combined these messages in a natural and more or less witty way. The first was a favorite of a salesperson who told me he used the same line with irate customers, fuming bosses, and fed-up wife. He would listen patiently to whatever verbal abuse came his way, and then, smiling slightly, would say, "Mr. Jones [Ted, Sally], I'm sure glad I got you on a good day." The usual result—a startled expression, followed by a slow smile and a chuckle. He would then embark on his version of "This really is important, and I'd really like to hear more about what you've got to say."

To appreciate our second example, you'll need to picture Trina, a youngish administrative manager, pitted against an all-male staff of engineers, machinists, and production workers whose job it was to turn out complex electrical devices. Trina, ordered to control costs, had been granted the authority to approve or disapprove all expenditures, a position that would not have made this young, attractive woman popular under any circumstances. It was not exactly a surprise, therefore, when senior engineers and no-nonsense foremen, irked at needing her okay on matters formerly within their own purview, escalated every budget discussion into a shouted denunciation of her ignorance, arrogance, and general stupidity. Although Trina stuck by her decisions from the start, she detested working in an atmosphere of flaring anger and intimidation, so, prompted by a half-remembered comic moment from a TV retrospective on silent film comedy, she hatched this ploy. First she requisitioned a library stool, that handy device about eighteen inches tall, used by librarians for quick access to top-shelved books—it should be mentioned here that she was a rather short person. Then, when a fuming manager charged uninvited into her cubicle, she would raise her hand, palm out, calmly push her chair back, stride around to the side of her desk, climb on the stool, and stand there nose-to-nose, arms at her side, head thrust forward, staring straight into the eyes of the shouter, attentive but not at all intimidated. The attacker would break up in laughter, hand her the piece of paper that had been the object of his wrath, and sit down to search, with her, for a businesslike resolution of their differences. After two weeks she was able to relegate her stool to a corner of her little office—a reminder that tiny can also be tough.

I like these examples because they demonstrate that your humor needn't be completely original, nor uproariously funny, to do its job. It needs only to highlight you as the strong yet completely reasonable person you are.

3

When Your Boss Isn't There for You: *The Artful Dodgers— Stallers, Wafflers, and Super-Delegators*

To do a good job in any organization, large or small, you must know where you're going, how much authority you have, and, at least from time to time, how well you're doing. Your boss is supposed to supply this information—it's known as giving direction—but unfortunately when the time comes to fulfill these managerial responsibilities, some bosses show a neat ability to avoid ever being on the spot. For such elusive fellows, who could be a more apt namesake than Dicken's nimble-footed hero—the Artful Dodger. Here are three such Dodgers in action.

CASE 1   By the time I first met forty-two-year-old George Hamilton, a business news reporter for a large metropolitan daily, his depression had eased off, and baffled resentment had taken center stage. This was his story:

> I've wanted a column of my own for years now. I'd substituted plenty of times for our regulars when they were sick, or hungover—always under their bylines, of course—and, until

37

two weeks ago, I thought I'd finally proved myself to Kate Bradshaw, our lovable business editor. It's finally penetrated my thick skull that the column is never going to happen. The awful part is that I wasted two years of my life trying to get her to decide yes or no. First, it was, "Not until the next budget year." Then it was, "Wait until Roger retires." Then it was, "We've had a cut in our department's budget." Then she wasn't sure exactly how to slant the new column and she had to talk it over with the managing editor. You know, if she had just told me that I didn't have the right style, that I was a boring writer, or that I was too dumb, I wouldn't have liked it, but at least I would have known where I stood. But she was never like that. I'd ask her whether I could handle a column, and she would assure me that I was fine, compliment me on some piece I'd recently done, and tell me that she was moving the column along as fast as she could. And stupid me, I believed her. Two weeks ago yesterday I woke up at two in the morning realizing that she is *never* going to make up her mind. I'm stuck in the newsroom for life, or else I move to another paper and start all over. What I can't figure out is how someone so indecisive could have gotten as far as she has in such a tough business.

CASE 2   Listen in on a conversation that took place one bright spring day between ace salesperson Fred Williams and his boss Sam Estaban, district sales manager for Armstrong Soap Products, Inc.

Fred: Sam, I'm really pissed about your handing over the best part of my territory to Stella, the new kid, and then saddling me with the poorest-producing county in the state. I'll have to start all over again building it up, and why the hell should I have to? I've proven myself for seven years and she's just starting out. For her to get the cream while I have to go back to slogging is a shitty deal and I don't like it.

Sam: Aw, you don't really mean that, Fred. You're so good— one of the best—opening up a new territory won't even be a real challenge for you. Besides, you know Wilma [the regional manager and Sam's boss]. She's really impressed with Stella's potential, and she wants to make sure that she doesn't get discouraged and leave.

Fred: Sam, I deserve to keep my old territory and I want it back. If it'll help, I'll talk to Wilma myself.

Sam: Well, sure, Fred, the last thing I want is you feeling done to. But I'd better be the one to talk to Wilma. Leave it to me. I don't think there'll be a problem.

Fred: Thanks Sam, I appreciate your taking it in the right way.

Exactly two weeks later, at 9:52 in the morning, Fred bursts into Sam's office and this conversation ensues.

Fred: Damn it, I thought you were going to let me keep my old territory. Wilma just stopped by to tell me how pleased she was that I was being "helpful" about Stella's move.

Sam: Well, I tried to talk to her two weeks ago, but I just couldn't get very far.

Fred: Why in hell didn't you tell me about that right away? I would have told her just how I feel about it. Now it's too late. Letters have already gone out to my customers telling them that Stella is their new salesperson. For a very sweet guy, Sam, you've screwed things up for me good.

Sam: Look, Fred, how about if we raise your guarantee for the next six months—would that help?

Fred: Sam, you can take your raise, and this job, and . . .

CASE 3   I had no sooner stepped through the door of Shirley Todd's office when she hit me with this torrent:

What burns me up the most about Sid [her boss] is the way he brags about what a great delegator he is. What that really means is that he expects me to read his mind about everything, and then if I guess wrong, that chickenheart just leaves me to hang out and dry. As an insignificant first-line supervisor, there's no way that I can be responsible for every policy decision. Don't get me wrong, I like having authority over my unit and I don't want a boss who insists on dotting all the i's. But, there's nothing worse than having to smell out which direction we're currently supposed to be going, and then being yelled at when I guess wrong.

With that, Shirley flipped a folded piece of paper at me. It was a handwritten note from the head of the mental health agency in which she worked, delivered that morning, she said, by Sid's secretary with a barely concealed smirk. The note was addressed to Sid, but Shirley was its unfortunate subject. The meaty part ran something like this:

> Your people *must* surely know that payments for rest and respite to families of severely disabled clients are *only* authorized when they *can't* afford occasional day care on their own. Since that policy has been clearly enunciated many times, I must conclude that Shirley Todd was trying to slip something through when she approved additional funding for the Jones family who are certainly not just scraping by. While I understand her sympathy for people who have to oversee an autistic child, I can't allow policies to be ignored, or worse, deliberately undermined. Please make sure that she is set straight.

After I had glanced through the note, Shirley said:

> Sid didn't even have the decency to tell me about this face to face, and tomorrow he'll act as if nothing happened. The frustrating thing is, the next time I ask him for some guidance on policies like that, all I'll get is some version of his standard response—"Whatever you think is right, Shirley." That is, if I can find him at all. The truth is he's never around when I need him.

Bosses like Kate, Sam, and Sid are never really there when you need them. They often have endearing qualities— they can be friendly, fair, sometimes idealistic. But when they are called upon to take a stand, to be forthright, to risk being unpopular, they disappoint and often disappear. Sure, if you're put upon by either of the brutes we encountered in the last chapter, you may feel a certain lack of sympathy for those who must endure almost the opposite. Yet, bosses who fade away just when you need a hand up, a firmly made decision, or honest and timely feedback, also add to their subordinates' load of aggravation, anger, and apathy. This chapter, then, is about leaders who don't lead, and how to best cope with them.

How to Recognize the Artful Dodgers: Stallers, Wafflers, and Super-Delegators

Artful Dodgers come in three varieties: Stallers (Kate), Wafflers (Sam), and Super-Delegators (Sid), all of whom abdicate vital areas of leadership. Stallers and Wafflers often look and act alike—although the sources of their difficult behavior are quite different—so we'll tackle them together. Later in the chapter, we'll get to Super-Delegators.

Both Stallers and Wafflers are immobilized by conflict, and they will seldom broach a topic that might provoke a strong negative reaction. (They often turn this into a virtue by pointing out, "You catch more flies with honey than with vinegar," or by blaming their lack of action on loyalty, or the wisdom of "causing no ripples.") As supervisors they are softies. They seldom upset you with negative comments about your performance, although they may hint or express indirectly that something is wrong. If you query them about how you're doing, they reassure you too much. You are left nervously wondering whether something might yet be amiss, without at all knowing what to do about it. What you seldom get is clear, specific, and unequivocal candor— "Sally, you made fourteen errors last month. Let's see if you can cut that in half this month." Instead, you are lulled with vague generalities: "Mrs. Jones wants us to improve our quality control. Let's see if we can't reduce our errors a little." They do this so well that you may not discover that some of the powers-that-be are soured on you until you are denied a promotion or are asked to leave.

Stallers and Wafflers are equally reluctant to set specific objectives, confront questions of priority, impose tight timetables, or be personally responsible for anything that makes life difficult for anyone. Although *their* bosses may establish concrete and specific goals, schedules, or standards, they will do little more than pass these on to you as burdens imposed by the people upstairs. In effect, although they would likely deny it, they have made their bosses your boss. But because they carefully guard their positions in the hierarchy—they are offended if you try to go around them— you may find yourself effectively placed in an organizational limbo. Your complaints about policies and procedures, justified or not, are sympathetically heard and then buried, or, worse, passed on in such watered-down form as to mark you as a complainer rather than an interested and responsible employee.

When, on occasion, they actually set objectives, or impose limits, they are usually couched in such general terms—"I wonder if we could improve our cost savings"— that you are never quite sure of the message's importance. Further, they seldom follow through, and since they haven't checked on how well the assignment is going, you may, with some logic, assume that it has lost whatever priority it might have once had. That is seldom the case. Often, without letting you in on what they are doing, they will have privately, and resentfully, taken care of it themselves.

Stallers and Wafflers often show commendable interest in the private lives, families, and career ambitions of those they feel responsible for. The warmth of that personal attention often induces their subordinates to patiently put up with the problematic behavior of such "thoughtful" bosses, long past the point at which they should have undertaken effective coping action.

To cope successfully with Stallers and Wafflers, it helps to understand what lies behind their frustrating behavior. Although they exhibit common behavior, what moves them to be difficult differs significantly, so here we'll take them up one at a time.

Understanding Stallers As individual contributors, Stallers work hard and genuinely enjoy being part of a team. They support their coworkers, listen well, and promote quality and high standards. With these sterling qualities and even moderate technical ability, it's not surprising that they were promoted to management. Having been so anointed with authority, however, Stallers are perpetually plucked at by a host of nagging dilemmas. Caring about others is wonderful, but when the one who cares is also a perfectionist who must, at times, say no to those for whom they care, the result is a continuing stress overload.* For example, if Stallers believe you are being mistreated by upper management, they feel inclined to loudly protest on your behalf. But wait—they also feel equally responsive to their superiors' appeals, spoken or silent, to keep the budget in hand, or prevent messy problems from surfacing. The result is equivocation, soothing words, and sleepless nights for the Stallers.

Unfortunately for you, Stallers most often deal with these conflicts by sidestepping them.

- *Staller's Dilemma*: If I'm candid with you about your poor performance, I'll distress you. If I'm not, I'm failing myself.
  Solution: Hint about your need to improve just enough to make you uneasy but not enough to get you to change.

- *Staller's Dilemma*: If you deserve a raise but my boss seems worried about money, I want to make it nice for both of you.
  Solution: Say to my boss, "It would be nice if Sally got the pay she deserves," say to Sally, "I tried, but there just isn't any money." Either way, I've avoided openly making anyone feel bad.

The reality that these scenarios are likely to lead to more, not less, distress is pushed out of awareness to that dark secret place where anxieties and tensions grow. Yes, there will be costs to all concerned in lost opportunities, and angry, demotivated employees. But awareness of these long-

---

* In counseling literature, this quality has recently been called codependence. Codependents often feel that it's up to them to make everything come out right for everyone, an impossible task for supervisors who must let others know when they are not performing up to standard. For those who would like to read further on the fascinating relationship between codependent supervision and its role in eliciting poor performance from subordinates, several sources can be found in the bibliography.

range losses simply can't compete with a Staller's urgent need to get out of an impossible emotional bind.

What to Avoid

It's tempting and logically appealing to counter a manager who isn't really there by dealing directly with one who is— your boss's boss. Or, if that's not feasible, why not move straight out on your own, taking action without waiting for anyone's approval? As understandable and appealing as these reactions may be, they are best avoided, at least until other coping attempts have failed. It's not that either of these approaches won't work in the short run. You may, indeed, wrest an "I guess so" from senior managers who assume that their assent is required because your boss is unavailable. The problems arise when you must present your boss with a fait accompli. The most common responses are an angry sulk, or worse, concealed irritation that later provokes a nasty display of temper. In other words, you will have turned your Staller into a brat or Fire Eater.

Coping With Stallers

The key to successfully coping with Stallers is to work harder than you should have to at helping them tell you what you really don't want to hear.

Make It Easy to Be Honest   Honesty, at least in the abstract, has much value to Stallers. Their impulses to be candid may be at war with their needs to help you remain in a constant state of comfort, but they do fervently believe people should always be honest with each other. Yet a direct suggestion that they might not be telling all is the least effective approach, for when you question their openness, you impede progress in two ways. First, you will likely provoke an attack of guilt, which seldom leads to productive action. Having punished themselves with an excruciating attack of remorse for their sins, they will, like most guilty people, be free to enjoy them again. Second, in their panic to protect you from yourself, they will insist they have indeed laid it all before you. No wonder that George, having pushed Kate for her honest opinion of his potential as a columnist, received hearty assurances that all was well.

Instead of questioning your boss's honesty, couch your need for direct and unambiguous information as a request for help. You might say, "What would help me the most, Kate, are some thoughts about how I might improve, even if I'm already doing pretty well." Several benefits come from putting it this way. Stallers believe in self-development, and they are motivated to help others in that effort. Then, too, by asking for "thoughts" you make it easier for your Staller to soften possibly harsh truths as relatively unimportant. You, however, will see them for what they are—hats in the door to test your capacity to absorb criticism. For that reason, it is vital that you respond to any bad news with a smile, a nod, and a reinforcing statement such as, "That's great," "Just the kind of thing I needed to hear," "I appreciate that," or, "Tell me more." Expect not to *feel* that way. You may agree that negative feedback is a necessary precursor to personal growth, but your trusty ego will rise to the occasion by telling you that none of the awful things you're hearing are more than minor, completely human, eminently forgivable foibles. Or, if you're having an attack of low self-esteem, you may simply feel exposed and worthless. While both are certainly common human responses, try not to reveal them. Tack on a bit of self-directed humor, for instance, to show that your defensiveness has not clouded your mature wish to see things as they are. Remember that codependents often treat others as helpless children who, regrettably, can't stand a little temporary discomfort for a longer-range gain. If you're seen as having a fragile ego, you will induce from a Staller boss the very behavior that you would like to stop. Similarly, be alert to signs that you may have been seduced into a dependent role.

Watch Your Tendency Toward Dependency Most human beings harbor a secret wish to feel protected and cared for as they were—or as they fantasize they were—as children. Its not surprising, then, that Stallers, effective codependents that they are, can seduce otherwise independent people into flirting with dependency. It usually happens something like this:

Employee: The purchasing agent has really been giving me a bad time. I made a little mistake in the model number when I ordered a replacement printer, and he yelled at me over the phone and then hung up.

Staller Supervisor: Yes, he really can be impossible sometimes. Do you want me to call him back?

Employee: Gee, I'd really appreciate it. I don't see how he gets away with talking to people that way.

It's always nice to have someone else pull one's irons out of the fire, and Stallers are usually quite gracious about it (although they may resent it later). But your acceptance of a dependent role can induce them to be protective even when it's against your long-term interest.

Bring Out Any Conflict They may not advertise the fact, but stalling managers are invariably bound up in a web of conflicting pushes and pulls. For example, they can find themselves caught between the wishes of *their* bosses for only good news and the legitimate gripes of their subordinates, or between competing appeals for scarce resources from equally deserving employees. Faced with such a dilemma—on one hand an employee who merits a salary increase and on the other an administration worried about salary costs—Stallers will often take no action at all, and then try to muddle the facts to both sides. The employee is assured that the delay is "probably a temporary cash-flow problem," while the purse holders are allowed to believe there aren't any "hardship" cases that would merit an exception to the "no raises right now" policy. Because most of us want to believe that all is well, all too often we collude in this confusion by welcoming these soothing reassurances with supportive nods and appreciative smiles.

A more effective approach is to help your Stallers move into action by asking them to make their conflicts explicit. Sometimes simply saying, "Kate, you seem to be having some doubts about which way to go, what's the conflict?" will do. However, you'll exert even more leverage by expressing at least one side of the conflict: "On one hand, right now we're in a budget push, what's on the other hand?"

It was this approach that finally tipped George to the main reason behind Kate's equivocation over his column. "Look, he said to her, "you've supported me all along in wanting to have a column of my own, but now I'm wondering whether I might be putting you in some kind of bind. On one hand, I know that you really want to help me out, what's the other side of it?" Kate's reply left him both relieved—at least he knew why he had been left dangling so long—and dismayed—he didn't at all like what he found out. Several years before, George had been overheard by Jerry, the current managing editor, loudly bragging about a reportorial exploit. To old-timer Jerry, George had appeared a shallow, self-centered upstart, and he had held tenaciously to that impression. While he never ordered Kate to fire George, his occasional quips about George's self-serving nature led Kate to believe that Jerry would never countenance a columnist guilty of such unprofessional grandstanding. She did not share her superior's belief that George was a "sensationalizer," but she respected Jerry's seniority and status and worried that promoting George's column might offend him.

Certainly George didn't like hearing about Jerry's opinion of him, but if he had not pried it out of Kate, he would not have been able to move beyond it.

Take a Consulting Role   Encouraging your Staller bosses to open up about flaws in your performance, or any other conflict they might feel, may be enough to get them moving. However, you can increase that likelihood by acting as a problem-solving consultant. Ask problem-solving questions, suggest alternatives, propose strategies, and in other ways help your boss do what he or she is being paid to do—solve problems and make decisions. You may resent it. If so, remind yourself that your object is to help yourself, not your Staller. Stallers facing conflict or the anticipation of distressing others will be in an emotional stew, but it is you who will bear the brunt of their feeling-fogged mentalities. Without some problem-solving help from you, they may take up permanent residence in the state of ambiguous evasion.

Provide Verbal Support Making important decisions is both tough and tiring for Stallers. So it pays to extend your personal support when they do. For example, when Kate raised the possibility of sounding out Jerry about a new business column, George said, "I want you to know, Kate, that I really think that that's a good idea." (Although it may seem a trivial distinction, I've found it useful to avoid the less personal forms of confirmation such as "It *was* the right thing to do," which may nudge Kate to wondering whether or not it "was," and dump her right back into her dilemma.) Agreement from a fellow human being steps up the odds that action will follow from a Staller's verbal commitment and good intentions.

Emphasize Quality and Service, Not Your Own Advancement Staller's high standards and concern for the welfare of others incline them toward projects and people with similar values. Insofar as you legitimately can, point out that you share those values, and present yourself as a person with a mature, community-oriented outlook. Above all, avoid sounding self-serving. Stallers tend to believe, at times to the detriment of their own advancement, that recognition will, at length, come to those who serve loyally and well. If you appear too impatient for promotion, or greedy for status or authority, you risk the withdrawal of whatever emotional commitment they may initially have felt.

But what if your immediate concerns *are* more for yourself than for the world at large? Should you try to hide your natural drive for success? Those are not easy questions. It's not that Stallers are difficult to fool; quite the opposite is true. People who trust are usually easy to lie to, and they are often taken advantage of. However, if they discover that their trust was undeserved, they are far more offended than their more cynical fellows might be, and then, often without a word to you, they will turn implacably aloof. In the long run, your best course would be to identify those aspects of quality and service you do believe in, and stick with them.

When Possible, Keep Stallers Out of the Decision Loop Because making unpopular decisions troubles them, Stallers are often relieved when others decide for them, and those "others" might as well be you. I don't mean to suggest that you ignore your Stallers or deny the importance of their ideas or positions. If they feel slighted by you, for example, if you gain their bosses' approval first, and then inform them of that fact, they will likely react first with hurt, then withdrawal or outright anger. The key is to use your boss as an information source or consultant. Plumb for facts, alternate possibilities, and potential risks, and having obtained this marvelous information, tell your boss as matter-of-factly as you can, "This has been a really helpful discussion; here's what I plan to do." Try not to let either your eyebrows or the pitch of your voice rise at the end of that sentence. Otherwise you may find that you've turned your brave statement into a querulous question—"Is that all right, boss?"

If, after you've promulgated your course of action, you encounter an objection, don't argue with it. Instead, act as if it were simply another bit of information from your wise consultant, and reformulate your plan to include the new issue. Having given you the benefit of their wisdom and experience, Stallers are usually quite willing to allow you to make the final decision.

Watch for Signs That You Are Pushing Too Hard   Imagine your Staller boss caught between two fires, badgered and beleaguered by two subordinates, perhaps, both clamoring for the same resource. If your boss runs true to Staller form, she will at first hang on to her equanimity, working hard for a peaceful solution. Then, if the fight continues, she will suddenly overload, lose control, and escape. The result is often an emotional, impulsive decision made by someone whose only concern is relief, always an unfortunate outcome for all concerned. Not only will the decision lack quality, but your Staller—having been once burned by it—will be twice reluctant to reconsider. At best, you can expect arm's-length execution, fault finding, and withdrawal of support in the face of even minor difficulties. Danger signals that emotional overload is imminent include: sudden irritation (your memo suddenly pitched across the table?), rapid pacing, an abrupt increase in foot swinging or other nervous mannerisms, a stiffened and immobile posture. When you detect signs that your boss's emotions may be boiling over, temporarily extricate both of you from the decision situation. Say something like "Look, Boss, let's continue this discussion about my raise tomorrow, I'm free at two o'clock." Your object will be to provide both a cooling-off period for your boss and breathing space for yourself. Then you can concentrate on determining what has provoked your boss's suddenly heightened stress.

In sum, Stallers promote your worst interest by plumping up your best interest. They sidestep direct unpleasant feedback; they only hint about your performance deficiencies. They collude with your wish that all will come out right, and thus they sweetly blind you to pitfalls. Worse yet, the more you show your frustration, the more your Staller will protect you from harsh reality with even more creative obfuscation. Certainly that was the fate of George Hamilton. The more he importuned Kate to promote him from reporter to columnist, the more "yes-buts" he gathered. Sure, budget and staffing problems frequently do waylay deserved promotions. But when initially reasonable assurances are followed by six months of inaction, a reassessment is in order—Am I just unlucky or am I being stalled? As painful as it may be, it's worthwhile testing your possibly rose-colored perspective by considering questions like these:

- Does your boss secretly doubt your ability? Do you recall overeffusive praise, or hints that while good, your performance could have been better?
- Are senior managers remembering the less competent you of several years ago? What, if anything, has been done to let them know you've changed?
- Is there another contender for that promotion on the scene? Does choosing between wonderful you, and that almost-as-wonderful competitor, have your boss in an irresolvable (for him, that is) conflict?

Your primary task is to discover the nature of your Staller's dilemma, so that you can best plan your next move, or even better, help your boss work it through to the right solution—promoting you, naturally.

Coping With Stallers in Action

About two weeks after he had learned that Jerry's antipathy toward him—ill-founded or not—had been the cause of Kate's reluctance, George called for an appointment, this time with a plan in mind. The conversation went something like this:

CRUCIAL CONVERSATION	COMMENT
George:	
Kate, I'm not sure I mentioned it before, but one reason I want this column is to give our readers some of the insider information I've acquired in the past ten years. You know I've been able to get behind the scenes a lot—learned about how things really work. I think that I can help people understand how to survive in the business jungle.	A good start—he shows Kate how and why he can help both the readers and the newspaper. And, as he remarked to me later—he realized that it was even true.

George:

Thanks, Kate. I do think that I can do the job, and that your decision will be good for the paper, and our readers, too. But I know that the only way that I'll keep developing is to get good, honest feedback from you.

George recovers pretty well. He does need to have Kate see him as a competent person.

He gives a better rationale for wanting her critical help.

Kate:

I'll drink to that.

Understanding Wafflers

On the surface, the behavior of Waffler Sam and Staller Kate seems almost identical. Both seemed supportive, both initially failed to stand up to their own bosses, and both left those they supervise feeling impotent and angry. Further, the crucial factor in both cases was dishonesty about important aspects of the situation.

Indeed, Wafflers, like Stallers, are also faced with a dilemma, but the divergent forces are quite different. While Stallers would like to be forthright, but are averse to distressing anyone, Wafflers simply want to be liked, approved of, and accepted by everyone, all the time. So, when their managerial roles push them to do things that are likely to make them unpopular—assigning employees to tasks they dislike, allocating resources unevenly, or recommending greater rewards for some than for others—they panic. Some resolve this dilemma by dividing all resources evenly regardless of need, allocating rewards without regard for performance, and passing off unpopular orders as the fault of higher-ups.

Others dance around the "I'm really a nice guy" predicament by proposing anemic compromises that satisfy no one. Similarly, they placate or distract those with grievances by kidding around or making light of the matter—anything to avoid tainting their "good kid" image.

Because Wafflers fear the loss of your approval, they need

help if they are to be honest. (Perhaps, they should be honest without your help, but they seldom will be.) Therefore the key coping step is to provide them with so much affirmation that they will feel confident enough to risk the truth.

How to Cope With Wafflers

Be Personal   Wafflers will waffle less if they feel personally accepted. For that reason, be personal with them. *Personal* does not mean *intimate* or *close*, but *courteous* or *cordial* aren't exactly on target either. Rather, being personal means doing a little extra to show your Wafflers that you regard them as likable human beings. Ask about weekend activities, chat about a favorite book or film, or suggest having lunch or coffee together. More than any protestations of friendliness, an invitation to shared activities, especially when they are not simply a part of the job, will convey the approval that Wafflers need. Actually, Wafflers usually *are* pleasant people who give others the kind of personal attention that I'm suggesting you return to them.

If the thought of carrying out this coping step is making your stomach ache or otherwise troubling you, consider these points before you reject the idea entirely:

1. If you are one of those people who, by nature or upbringing, approaches life in an orderly, rational way, you are also likely to feel less comfortable with the quirky, nonrational side of people. Consequently you may have forgotten that some others want—need, actually—more personal support and attention than you do, if they are to function well.
2. Because bosses are expected to give recognition and praise when due, it is sometimes forgotten that they also may have unmet needs for recognition and praise, and there is nothing inappropriate about subordinates satisfying them.
3. If your boss has waffled away your raise, or, as in the case of Fred, your well-developed sales territory, you

may not feel much like being personal, in a friendly way, that is. If so, remind yourself that coping, when it works, is usually better than quitting.

Don't Fight Compromise A Waffler's obsession with good relationships has a positive side—a passion for positive compromise in which all parties to a conflict come away with something they value. The great appeal to Wafflers of this sort of win-win strategy is that if it's carried off with polish and a bit of humor, no one ends up sore at anyone else. For that reason, accepting, or better yet proposing, a compromise even when you're certain you have a right to fully receive what you've requested, can turn a potential disaster into a partial win. If you continue to fight, you risk driving your Waffler into hiding—"Let's talk about it later," or into a primitive defense in which you discover that Wafflers pushed too far can sometimes turn into Fire Eaters. Instead, make clear your objections, but suggest a compromise, such as, "I still believe that it was my right to hang on to my old territory, but since the transfer has already been made, a really hefty guarantee will give me time to build up the new territory."

Similarly, when your boss is trying desperately to give you bad news—keeping it light, perhaps as Wafflers are wont to do—"Well, Aggie, it's a good thing you're rich, because the word is going around that nobody gets any raises"—you can cut through the sweetness and light and yet not put your boss out of commission with an "Okay, Alex, but is there any way to compromise?" Console yourself with the knowledge that one small victory can be a stepping-stone to others, and, anyway, it's almost always better than no gain at all. Even more important, a compromise may be the only way to keep your boss functioning in a disagreeable situation.

Finally, bear in mind that the best way for fearful people to make progress is to take one small step at a time, then check for catastrophe. If none has occurred, another small step can be chanced, and so on. While Wafflers intellectually know that, when faced with a fight, they often forget. So, it's worthwhile to remind them, and to help plan a strategy that will maintain reasonably good relations and also help you get at least some of what you want.

Coping With Wafflers in Practice

Let's see how Fred fared when he tried these coping methods with his waffling boss, Sam.

CRUCIAL CONVERSATION	COMMENT
Fred:	
Damn it, Sam, I just finished reading your note about giving part of my sales territory to Stella and then adding that poor-ass Wentworth County to my territory to make up for it.	Fred tries to be matter-of-fact but it's hard not to sound angry when you've been unexpectedly zapped.
Okay, okay, I'm sure there was a good reason for your doing it. I know you've always been fair, and you do what you can for your hardworking salespeople.	Nice recovery, Fred. (One look at Sam's face told him that his anger was panicking Sam.)
What might make me feel better is knowing some of the reasons behind this move.	Good thinking, Fred. While Sam is explaining, you get a breather.
Sam:	
You know how much I appreciate your work, Fred. Why, you're the best salesperson around. That's why Wilma thought that you wouldn't mind if we gave part of your better-developed territory to Stella. We think she could become a really great salesperson, and we want to make sure that she doesn't get discouraged and leave.	Notice how neatly Sam dumps all the blame on Wilma.

Fred:

Well, Sam, I have to tell you that I'd really rather not do this. I was looking forward to profiting by all of the hard work that I've put in. I could write all my customers and tell them that I'm still their man.

Personal appeals work better on Wafflers than logical arguments.

Look, would it be tough for you to go back to Wilma and tell her that you've changed your mind?

Fred acknowledges the bind Sam is in.

Sam:

Yeah, she seemed pretty enthusiastic about this move. Actually—I don't know if I should really be telling you this—but Stella is the daughter of one of Wilma's sorority sisters and Wilma was looking for a way to give her a boost without hurting the company's sales.

Now the real reasons begin to emerge.

Fred:

Sam, I really appreciate your telling me that. I can see why that's a tough situation for you to deal with. How about this? Put the area around Centerville back into my territory—I've really busted my ass to build up our accounts there. And also can you work out some way to keep my compensation up until I get the new territory in line?

Fred resists the impulse to say "Whaaaat?" Instead, he keeps Sam in a realistic mode with a positive comment. Then he proposes a compromise that he can live with.

Sam:

Well, sure—I can up your guarantee for six months, but I don't know how Wilma would feel about Centerville . . .

Sam begins to waffle a bit.

Fred:

Here's what I'd like to do, Sam. I'd like to meet with Wilma myself—you're welcome to be there, of course. I can offer to help Stella out in getting to know that part of my territory she *will* get, and I can make the case for Centerville myself.

Fred to the rescue.

Sam:

You won't mention anything about sorority sisters will you?

(You may be wondering why such a weakling was promoted. Because the same qualities that produce a Waffler are often found in top salespeople. Unfortunately, top salespeople don't always make top supervisors.)

Fred:

Now Sam, you know me better than that. Would I do anything to cause trouble for as nice a boss as you?

A pat on the back for Sam, who was honest above and beyond his comfort zone.

Super-Delegators

If one looked only at what they said, Super-Delegators would seem wonderful examples of good management practice. Most of them are quite vocal about their interest in "letting people run their own show." Doesn't every management text imply that the solution to most organizational problems, from time management to disastrous decisions, is delegation and more delegation?

But even so sterling a practice as delegation can be over-applied. In the case of Super-Delegators, it's not so much a matter of pushing too much delegation, as it is using it inappropriately and unskillfully.

For example, while Super-Delegators are usually quite willing to enumerate general goals, they tend to be casual about the specifics that count—priorities, the standards by which your performance will be judged, or guidelines for resolving sticky policy questions. If, however, your decisions, or the way you have implemented them, don't meet your Super-Delegators' expectations—the ones that they neglected to tell you about—you may find that you have not only lost their support, but they have sided with their own bosses, or with accusing customers or clients, in targeting you as the villain. Here's how one subordinate of a Super-Delegator put it:

> My boss Bob thinks he's an expert delegator. It's true that he leaves me completely alone once he's given me an assignment. That part is fine, or it would be if he would really let me in on what he expects, and why he's asked me to do it. But he doesn't. He'll buck me a memo from someone else with a scribbled "Would you take care of this, Bill." If I plow ahead on my own, half the time it turns out that he had a completely different idea about it. Or I'll run into some static from people whose toes I've stepped on, only to find out that he knew there might be some tender toes around. According to him, it's my job to find out about things like that, but if I do go check with him before I get started, he'll patronize me as if I were a kid who had to be told to put his shoes on before he laces them up. Oh, Bob's a real expert all right—at getting across that he wonders why in the world he ever made me his deputy.

Understanding Super-Delegators

Three factors combine to turn Super-Delegators' ardor for delegation into a dismaying experience for their subordinates: An incomplete knowledge of the delegation process, a wish for more personal freedom of action than most managerial roles allow, and an erroneous perception that others are as impatient with any sort of managerial direction as they. For a smaller group of Super-Delegators, a fourth factor is the culprit, a disquieting suspicion that they may not be worthy enough to direct the affairs of others.

Incomplete Delegation   Super-Delegators confuse delegation with "dumping." They have not yet grasped the fact that any delegation ought to include a clear delineation of expected results, as well as the constraints within which the delegated task should be accomplished, and how much authority was, in fact, delegated.

Mistakenly confident that they are first-rate managers, because they are super delegators, it's not hard to understand why Super-Delegators blame their subordinates for missteps, late or incomplete assignments, and lack of follow-through.

Don't Fence Me In   Most Super-Delegators relish having a large yard to play in. They do the best they can to keep their own bosses at arm's length so that they can freely choose how and where to spend their time. They are often involved in projects that have little direct relevance to the major tasks for which their part of the organization is charged. For example, they take on time-consuming leadership roles in professional or trade organizations, are part owners in outside businesses, or become heavily involved in personal development programs. While these "sidelines" have much to commend them, when they siphon off a significant portion of a manager's time and attention, other things must suffer. Those "things" are often the staff members who need perspective, timely information, or guidelines if they are to do a first-rate job.

"I'll Be Back in a While"   Super-Delegators don't want supervision from their own bosses, and they assume that you feel the same way. The net result is that Super-Delegators are often quite literally not there. To compound the problem, because even *they* have doubts about the full propriety of their personal projects, they are often vague

about where they are going, and how they might be reached
if others need to confer with them.

Impatient With Supervision   Super-Delegators tend to
be rapid-fire thinkers who quickly size up situations, make
confident decisions with few second thoughts, and charge
off to fix whatever needs fixing. Naturally they presume that
other smart people think about things as they do, and they
are genuinely surprised when their hasty, incomplete directions leave some of those bright others feeling inadequately
briefed and unsure of what to do. Their obvious confidence
that they have been as informative as any self-assured person ought to expect, often deters subordinates from asking
useful questions. After all, if your boss seems to be judging
you on the amount of "initiative" and "self-direction" you
show, it's easy to be convinced that you really "should"
puzzle it all out for yourself.

Coping With Super-Delegators

The essence of coping with Super-Delegators is to simultaneously induce them to spell out just enough so that you
are no longer floundering, while taking full advantage of the
freedom of action that such bosses provide. You will have to
take the initiative, since they are certain that they are managing well. Without a little nudging from you, it is probably
futile to expect that they will try to improve. The most
useful kinds of nudging are telling them how you would
like to be supervised, and negotiating a variety of mecha-
nisms that will keep you in touch, without either of you
giving up much independence of action.

Let Them Know How You Want to Be Supervised   Most
of us believe that what we want from supervisors (or from a
parent, spouse, or child, for that matter) is what any sensible person would want, and is therefore self-evident. Then,
when we are not treated as we expect to be treated, we are
disappointed and, too often, we ascribe their derelictions to
thoughtlessness, incompetence, or some other personal foi-

ble. The fact is that unless we inform them otherwise, most people will treat us as *they* would like to be treated, which may not be at all to our liking. For that reason, it's *always* useful to negotiate mutual expectations with anyone important to you—and bosses certainly are. Super-Delegators are usually willing to engage in such a discussion if, naturally, it does not require much time or attention from them. Broach it informally as "a few things that I'd like you to do that would help me to do my job better." Among the things you'll ask for are a clarification of your true level of authority, more one-on-one meetings, and an agreement on how soon you can expect your boss to respond to notes or phone calls. (You'll find a fuller discussion of how to negotiate expectations in chapter 7.) In other words, instead of letting your evanescent boss set the pattern for keeping in touch, you'll ask for the minimum you need to do your job, but no more than the minimum. Here are some particulars.

Negotiate Your Level of Authority   Even if the language of organizational discourse was not invented to confuse the people it was supposed to enlighten, it has been markedly successfully in doing just that. Among the most iniquitous of these "flexible" expressions are "coordinate," "in charge of," "leading role," and "it's your bailiwick." For example, have you ever been told that you are "in charge of the mailroom" only to discover that your "decision" to limit expensive overnight mail has been countermanded by a higher authority. Obviously, "in charge of" did not mean "full authority to manage." It must have meant, or so you assumed, only the right to make procedural decisions of a limited kind and size—what kind and which size were up to you to find out. At that point you may have chosen to follow the "sensible," if self-diminishing, course of pushing every decision back up the chain of command. If you were less sensible but more persistent, you would have continued to test until, having run into enough walls, you work out what you can decide and what you can only recommend. Clearly it's particularly important to know your level of authority when you have a boss who is seldom around or—as in the instance of Shirley, whose plight began this chapter—one who blithely assumes that the mantle of authority was really fully passed on. Shirley believed that Sid's sincerely delivered "You're in charge of casework decisions" meant that she could decide when policy exceptions were warranted. She was wrong. If she had thought to ask a few clarifying questions, such as "Are there limits?" she might have saved herself a slightly tarnished reputation and some bruised feelings.

To be sure, Super-Delegators are often impatient with such questions, believing that they limit freedom of action. And to some extent they do. The point that such bosses miss is that complete freedom is illusory, if, as in Shirley's case, restrictive conditions actually exist. When you ask "What's my level of authority?" you merely make those restrictions visible.

Coax Out Guidelines   If your boss later disagrees with decisions you've made, get in the habit of asking about the thoughts behind that different decision. For example, after she had recovered from her initial pique, Shirley asked Sid:

Are there any circumstances in which you might approve child-care money for a family as well off as the Joneses?

What are the factors that you apply when deciding whether a middle-class family should get extra "time off" money?

If Sid's responses had been too general to be especially enlightening—"Well, that might depend on what I thought might happen if they didn't get a chance to get away for awhile," she would need to be ready to probe further. Most people are not consciously aware of the criteria that guide their decisions, but those guidelines are invariably there and they can be coaxed out with a little effort. Shirley might have helped Sid be more specific with, "Are you saying that exhaustion in the family is one thing you look for?" True, if he had been a thoughtful supervisor, and not a Super-Delegator, he would have done all this as part of a formal delegation order to Shirley. But the motivation and qualities of mind of most Super-Delegators make them see such niceties as unnecessary embellishments, since "It's all a matter of good judgment." Once again, the essence of coping with difficult people, bosses or not, is moving past that understandable thought, "Why do *I* have to make him do what he should be doing anyway." Once you've recognized that Sid does what he does because of who he is, and it is that "who" with which you have to cope, doing what you need to do to get what you want becomes a practical matter rather than a moral issue.

A Time to Meet   Scheduled one-on-one meetings can provide a way to temporarily anchor down your Super-Delegator. Like most people with busy schedules, you may be reluctant to give up more time to meetings, but consider the advantages. Managers seldom turn down requests for meetings with individual staff members. It's hard to come up with honorable reasons for not acceding to that request, especially when your subordinate gives reasons for wanting the meeting. Hard-to-turn-down reasons include a need for briefings on projects, a wish to coordinate with relevant activities of other staff members, or a need to use your boss as a consultant or coach. (Super-Delegators have large egos and are usually flattered by your recognition of their talents. They may not want to *do* anything, but they are quite willing to talk about it.) Unfortunately, while Super-Delegating bosses may readily agree to meet with you, the meeting schedule can quickly erode because of their wide-ranging interests. Don't take this as a sign that it was a poor idea, simply ask that a new time and place be set each time a meeting has been canceled or "postponed."

Agree on Turn-Around Time   Since Super-Delegators' interests are wide and scattered, they are often remiss in returning phone calls and messages. While you can't force your boss to return your calls within a day, you can *ask* that it be done. Keep in mind that it's usually to your advantage to settle for a response interval that your boss can actually live with, even if you would prefer something shorter. After all, having an approximation of how soon you will get a reply is usually more important than the length of the turn-around time.

Another Breed of Super-Delegators: the Self-Doubters

Thus far we've dealt with Super-Delegators who have an antipathy to being closely supervised themselves, and a belief that everyone has the same disinclination. However, there is another breed whose hesitancy at providing direction stems from a quite different source. It is a suspicion—sometimes justified, sometimes not—that those whom they are supposed to direct are actually more competent than they. I've especially noted this professional diffidence in managers with narrow expertise who have been put in charge of informed colleagues, or specialists from a multitude of fields. Similarly, managers junior in age or experience are often reluctant to direct others who are, if not brighter, at least more senior than themselves.

Why not simply write off such retiring bosses? Do you really want or need the support of a manager whose knowledge of your business is less than your own? Probably not, when only technical matters are in question. However, power and influence are often the basic ingredients of project funding, raises, and promotions. It is the degree and kind of managerial support that usually determines who gets scarce prizes. For that reason alone, it's worthwhile to try to increase a self-deprecating boss's store of confidence. Sure, you could run your own verbal interference, but you risk having your best arguments discounted as self-serving. Your boss, if he or she is not perceived as a nonentity, or little more than a message pipeline, can more convincingly than you plump for your "really great idea."

I have often encountered a sad scenario in which scientific or technical "stars" dismissively undercut their less renowned bosses. Prodded by their own egos, and resentful that they must, at least nominally, report to nonentities of inferior talent, they ignore, insult, and openly disparage their bosses. When this happens, everyone loses, for goal and priority setting, coordination, and, most important, representation in the ubiquitous fight for resources, are vital to the success of any venture. Those fruits of sound management seldom come from insecure, diffident leaders.

Coping With Self-Doubters   The key to coping with Self-Doubters is to understand that you must grant them permission to be active managers. Doing so might sound something like this:

> John, I really appreciated your mentioning that "program flexibility" is the new buzzword upstairs. I added a few introductory paragraphs to my project request, and it was approved when most of the other proposals were sent back. Maybe you ought to bring that kind of briefing into our quarterly staff meetings? In addition, I'd like to have you review all of my requests for additional funding. It might trigger ideas like that one, and also make it easier for you to handle questions from on high.

Without complaining, scolding, or lecturing, you've suggested how your self-doubting boss *has* helped, and you have invited the sort of direction that you believe he or she can, and ought to, provide.

Turn Super-Delegation Into an Asset

Having propped up your Self-Doubter, clarified just what you are in charge of, and negotiated a workable system for keeping in touch, you may find that working for a Super-Delegator is, in balance, an asset. A confusing absence of direction has been transformed into an enviable freedom to maneuver and a real chance to demonstrate your capabilities.

4

When Your Boss Holds the Reins Too Tightly: *Power Clutchers, Paranoids, and Perfectionists*

Most of us relish the glow that follows skillful accomplishment. But when our supervisors hold the reins of their authority too tightly—making every decision, directing every move—the opportunity for solid achievement just isn't there. Here are two examples of what it's like to be on the receiving end of this kind of stultifying supervision. As you'll see, power-clutching managers can be found at any organizational level.

Allen Payton was explaining to me why he was planning to resign from the executive position he'd worked so hard to get the year before:

> When I first began to talk to John Sturges [his boss] about this job, I was impressed by both his tremendous knowledge of the business and the care with which he had dug up a lot of information about me. He was obviously not a man given to slapdash decisions and I felt that I could count on what he told me. What I didn't count on was that the CEO of a growing five-hundred-million-dollar company would pick an experienced executive to head his most important divi-

sion, and then treat him as if he were still in the first grade. Every decision—product mix, markets, which R & D projects to keep or to dump, who I should promote, who I should fire—decisions that I or my own subordinates should be making, must have his approval. If I try to disagree with him, he pretends to listen for awhile but then he keeps after me until I just get tired of resisting. After all, he *is* the CEO and he has a *right* to decide everything. Don't mistake me—he's a very smart man with good ideas and an enormous store of knowledge. But I want a chance to show what I can do at this level, and I'll never get it working for John.

Allen paused for an instant, looking down at the palms of his hands. Then he said:

The real reason I'm quitting is that for the last six months I've stopped caring about what he does. I go through the motions, I collect my twenty-thousand-a-month salary, and I let him run the whole thing. Two months ago I heard myself tell two of my best people that they might as well send their reports directly to John with a copy to me, since he was going to make the final decisions anyway. When they left my office I realized that if I don't get myself out soon, I might stay here forever.

Here is Rita's description of her boss, Richard Lee, an accounting manager:

Richard is really a very nice man, soft-spoken, even gentle. But the way he checks every single invoice that I've already okayed for payment, makes me wonder why I'm even here at all. Two months ago, I got mad and asked him about it. He just went into a long song and dance about how that was part of his job and he did that with everyone. That part is true, but that doesn't mean it's the right thing to do. What is particularly infuriating to me is that, two or three times a month, he will single out a particular invoice, usually a big one, and want to see all of the assorted paperwork that backs it up. Once he even called the vendor to check on the amounts. When I ask him about those, he just clams up and changes the subject. The pay is very good at this place, and the fringe benefits are even better. Otherwise I don't think I would stay. Nobody likes being treated as if they were either incompetent or dishonest, or maybe both.

The behavior of Power Clutchers is similar regardless of the habitat in which they are found. Most people who complain about their too closely supervising bosses mention one or more of these three not unrelated behaviors:

- They tell you precisely what, when, how and with whom you are to do your job.
- They insist on finalizing decisions that should be made by you or by your subordinates.
- They delegate wide responsibility to you—or at least they say they do—but then proceed to commit either one or the other of the preceding sins, and sometimes both, in the most important and interesting areas of your job.

Common reactions to such close supervision are an acute sense of being stifled, and either resignation, with a lessening of self-regard, or an angry flight into incompetence with the flavor of: "Okay, buster, if you're so smart you can do it all!" This series of understandable reactions simply verifies to the Clutcher that those tight controls were indeed justified. As John Sturges, Allen's nondelegating nemesis, put it, "When Allen didn't even care enough about what was going on to attend his own department heads' meetings, I really began to wonder if I'd found the right person for that responsible a job."

Understanding Power Clutchers

Although power clutching is usually the result of a complexity of motivations, there here are several common reasons why some managers hold the reins too tightly: a need to be certain, lack of confidence and trust, an irrational search for perfection, and an overstrong wish to be in charge.

A Need to Be Certain   Arthur Lane was a senior government auditor for a large East Coast city. He supervised a group of highly experienced auditors who were given the dual task of reporting problems in the agency being investigated to the city manager's office, and suggesting needed improvements to the various agency heads. In theory, each auditor was delegated wide freedom of action, working almost independently under the guidance of the senior auditor. However, Arthur, conscientious to the ultimate degree, had his own interpretation of "guidance." He not only insisted on reviewing every recommendation proposed by his journeymen auditors, but he also inspected in detail the findings on which those recommendations were based. Not surprisingly Arthur's superiors were constantly at him because of the length of time it took his unit to complete its audits. They suspected—correctly as it turned out—that it was his insistence on reviewing everything that was causing the delay.

Several times Arthur had been asked to cut down on his duplicative reviews. Each time he had listened respectfully, without comment, and then proceeded to continue as he always had. He readily admitted to me, that his audits took longer than anyone else's, and therefore cost the city about half again as much as had been budgeted. He insisted, however, that there was nothing he could do about it, because it was a manager's job to ensure that everything was correct. He buttressed his point by showing me four factual errors that he had caught and, even worse, he said, was the poor judgment of two of his auditors who had not suggested changes that Arthur believed were probably warranted by their findings:

"I have to sign my name to every final report," he firmly pointed out, "and there's only one way that I can honestly do it—make sure that it's been done right. Just because everyone else is willing to do a slipshod job, does not mean that I should," were Arthur's final words.

While Arthur was careful to an extreme, I have found that many overcontrolling managers do indeed believe they are only doing what any responsible person should. Often they are supported in this notion by bureaucratic procedures that seem to question whether anyone below the rank of CEO should be permitted to finalize even the most innocuous decision. Arthur, who was far from stupid, rested his case by pointing to the boldface notation just above the box set aside for the senior auditor's signature. "I certify this report to be correct" said it all, Arthur's gesture clearly implied. "How can I sign my name to that," he insisted, "if I don't *know* that it is correct?"

Most of our ideas about how supervisors should supervise are formed from observations of our own first supervisors, who were often our parents. That would be all to the good if we simply mimicked what we liked, or what seemed to work, and avoided what we didn't. But we humans are queer creatures. Just as some parents at age thirty-five often find themselves replicating parental behaviors they couldn't stand at age fifteen, so do some managers repeat the irksome performance of their supervisory role models. Although they may read modern texts on supervision and even intellectually agree with them, it's hard to shake the pictures in their minds that tell them that someone in charge ought to be in full control. By insisting that managers know in detail what each individual under their supervision is doing, senior executives often exacerbate the problem. While their words may endorse the concept of pushing decision making down to the lowest organizational level, their grim visages, when subordinate managers are not completely up on all that is happening in their units, communicate that such uncertainty is a sign of lax management. In that milieu, only a fool would not conclude that mistakes are unforgivable, and that those-who-must-be-pleased will not tolerate the occasionally variant judgments, or wavery facts, that are a necessary consequence of delegation to an unequally talented group of employees.

Different Means Defective   Most of us don't think much about how we think, so it's often a surprise to discover that there is an impressive array of evidence that individuals think about things in quite different ways. For twelve years, my colleagues and I have studied the impact of those thinking-style differences on interpersonal effectiveness and team functioning, and at least two realities seem well demonstrated. If you and your boss are a part of the 85 percent of people who rely on only one or two styles of thinking, and the styles you prefer are not the same, you are likely to see each other as confused, incompetent, and "resistant" to what each of you knows is an obviously good idea. That circumstance is unfortunate because, in general, the greater the variety of thinking styles brought to bear on a problem, the more realistic and useful will be the solution. Secondly, your boss, doubting your competence, will be inclined to worry about your clearly muddled mentality and try to contain it by allowing you a minimum of decision-making responsibility. For example, some people—Arthur is certainly one—value accuracy, thoroughness, and an orderly approach to just about anything. Others, both blessed and cursed with less perfectionist qualities of mind, value rapid—Arthur would say hasty—action that gets things running again with a minimum of fuss. From that perspective, it's not difficult to see why Arthur believed that Bud Adams, one of his auditors, needed judicious supervision. True, Bud had been inordinately successful at getting department executives to take action on many of his recommendations—which puzzled Arthur, but he attributed it to luck and the equally illogical ways of many line managers. "You can talk about delegation all you want," said Arthur, "but how can I place confidence in someone like Bud, who bases his recommendations solely on informal conversations with a few front-line workers? That's just not the way an auditor should do business."

Lack of Trust   Some people are perennially suspicious of others. Perhaps they were lied to or cheated in the past and are determined never again to play the patsy. Or they may have been indoctrinated to distrust others by parents, teachers, or other figures important in their lives. Saddest of all are the positive souls who idealistically believe that everyone ought to be considered trustworthy. When others have proven them wrong by taking advantage of their naïveté, they are the slowest to forgive. Then, subsequently hearing from their subordiantes, "I worked hard on this report all weekend, but I still couldn't get it done," their inner voices shout, "You believed someone once, how do you know you're getting the truth now?"

Then there are those with a touch of paranoia. Normal in most circumstances, they can become extraordinarily suspicious when their delusional enclaves are entered. At various times I've encountered individual managers who became sick with worry about plots to rig employee travel expenses, overtime hours, promotional opportunities, and even relationships with the media. Dealing with others whose behavior has exceeded the bounds of normalcy is invariably disturbing, especially when there is an unexpected switch from easy camaraderie to exaggerated suspicion.

Salesperson Gina Scott put it this way: "Harry [her boss] has given me the authority to offer my customers discounts that could cost the company thousands of dollars, but when he gets my monthly travel-expense claim, he badgers me about each and every item. He's called taxi companies to check on what the fare should have been, and he made me show him—not tell him, show him—just how many special-order pages I had typed up at a hotel secretarial service. Just last week he asked me what I ate to justify a dinner claim of twenty-four dollars at a Chicago hotel. Sure, I know taxi drivers do hand out blank receipt forms—well, it's no skin off their teeth—but how can he trust me with the company's good name and then make such a big deal out of trivialities? Hell, if I wanted to gouge the company, I could make a kickback deal with a discounted customer for a lot more bucks than I could get out of exaggerating a taxi fare. I put up with it because in most ways he's a pretty good boss, but when he gets rabid about expenses, I'll tell you—it's weird."

Perfectionist Panic　It's easy enough to delegate when you're the kind who can take mistakes in stride. Dropping the ball a few times is part of the game, you tell yourself, it's the main chance not the details that count. You're right, of course, but for some people, loosening their grip on work for which they're responsible is an exercise in perpetual panic. They are haunted by the specter of imperfection, sure that if they don't personally oversee every aspect of each task, terrible things will happen. It was their misfortune to be the product of loving parents who implanted in them an irrational dilemma, "If I don't do things perfectly, then I'm a failure." (A close relative is: "If I don't have total control, then I have no control.")

While there is a modicum of sense in such beliefs—mistakes *can* sometimes be costly—they are largely non-sense. Human beings have never demonstrated perfection in either character or behavior, and, in contrast, occasional failure has invariably been a characteristic of outstanding achievers. Unrealistic as they are, such beliefs place conscientious bosses in an untenable position. The only way they can stave off failure and ensure that everything is exactly as it should be, is by doing it all themselves. Yet, they are often intellectually aware that they are not perfection itself, or even the most capable person around. So they clutch at every detail because—as with their buggy-driving namesakes—a tight hand on the reins to some extent alleviates the constant worry that their perfect control will be lost. When, despite all their efforts to keep on the path of perfection, their team stumbles a bit—often because it was denied the opportunity to think for itself—they panic. An immediate reaction is to scold, or fire a volley of emotional whys at anyone in the immediate vicinity of the error. Soon, however, they can't stand the anxiety and they tighten their grip even more, double-checking every invoice, report, and order, and making every presentation. Invariably they will take more time to accomplish less—pushing a buggy that is dragging a bewildered team that should be pulling it is slow work. Exhausting, too.

The Drive for Power   Studies of what makes a manager effective have shown that a constant inner nudge to become powerful and influential is almost indispensable, and, indeed, almost every manager who is successful has it. As you might expect, the *most* productive executives channel their needs for power toward organizational, rather than personal, goals, and prefer rational persuasion and joint problem solving to employee bashing. Unfortunately, for too many otherwise enlightened managers, the joys of a "power high" are more than a match for fleeting thoughts that more delegation might make them better managers.

Peter Melton was deputy director of a small state agency. He met regularly with his department heads to plan their activities for the week, routinely checked with them to see how well the plans were being carried out, and loudly took those same department heads to task when anything went wrong. Just another of those "afraid to let it go" people we've just visited? Not at all. Peter was an energetic, articulate, well-educated manager, who had maybe a little too much self-confidence. He also thoroughly understood the value of delegation—at least he had convinced me he did— and had more than enough trust in the ability of his subordinate managers to have delegated appropriately to them. When I asked him why he did not, he grinned, just a touch wickedly, and said, "Sure, they could do it all, they are very smart people, but I just have a lot of fun running things. I enjoy thinking things through, I enjoy arguing them into seeing my side of the question, and if I were to tell all, I'd admit that I really enjoy making them do things my way, even when they think I'm wrong. I suppose they'd all rather be running the show instead of me, but, hell, they have plenty of leeway supervising their own people."

People like Peter Melton enjoy feeling powerful. True, the way he satisfied his wish to always be dominant had several unfortunate outcomes. His department heads were as bright as he thought they were, and they resented what they took to be a lack of confidence. More than that, because their "discussions" with Peter often deteriorated into "my way" or "your way" arguments, his staff did not propose useful compromises simply to avoid another "fruitless battle of wills."

Coping With Bosses Who Don't Delegate

The key to coping with bosses who won't, can't, or don't delegate is a martial-arts approach. Use the energy that drives your opponent, your tight-reining boss, to help you gain the upper hand—a level of delegation appropriate to your job and capabilities. Rather than trying to overcome the inner forces that have prevented your boss from relinquishing tight control, you'll flow with them. For instance, you won't try to turn an apprehensive boss into a risk taker—a nice thought, perhaps, but likely outside the range of possibility. Lacking compelling force or tempting rewards, efforts to *make* others do what they've been taught not to do, or prevent them from doing what they love to do, are doomed to both frustration and failure. Rather, you will show a fearful boss that empowering you will further secure him from attack by whichever goblins are presumed to be lurking in the organizational wings. Similarly you won't attempt to talk a slightly paranoid boss out of being suspicious, when the more you say "trust me," the less likely you are to be trusted. Instead, you'll show your boss how to monitor your work so trust won't be necessary.

Keep in mind in reading through the suggestions that follow that you'll need to emphasize certain methods more than others, depending upon your best guesses about what is causing your boss to hold the reins too tightly.

Uncover Hidden Doubts About Your Competence or Trustworthiness It's always wise—if unpleasant—to stay alert for clues that there is something in your own performance that makes your boss reluctant to give you more freedom. Overlong silences, abrupt changes of topic, the use of "weasel-ly," phrases such as, "Your work is *generally* on target," "I'm mostly pleased with how things are going," are always worth following up. Set an inviting, nondefensive tone—"If things have happened in the past that make you doubt my ability to use more authority, it would help me a lot to hear about it, even if it's not anything big." Then wait. If something is forthcoming, listen attentively, refrain from making excuses or even explaining why you did whatever you've been accused of doing. Instead, say, "This is really helpful," and ask for more. Steady your inner desire to deny it all by dwelling on your purpose for all this masochism, to enable your boss to put into words what he or she is already thinking. Having heard the worst first, acknowledge your boss's concern, whether or not you agree with the allegations—"I can see that you've had some doubts about the way I handle money," then point out how you plan to prevent such things from happening again— "that's just the reason why I've taken these financial-planning courses over the last year." If you haven't been that aware of the problems your boss has pointed to, it can't hurt to ask how you might have more effectively handled them. Several studies have shown that most bosses enjoy demonstrating to their subordinates how wise they are and often feel hurt that they are seldom asked for that wisdom, so you may convince your bosses of your own perspicacity by recognizing theirs.

Look More Competent by Communicating to Your Boss's Strengths   Recall from our earlier discussion of thinking styles that *different* often means *defective*. You can reduce this possibility by pushing your proposals at your bosses in ways that fit the channels of their minds. To do this you'll have to get a rough fix on which modes of thinking and problem solving they use most frequently. Take a few moments right now to place your boss in one or two of these five thinking-style categories. Keep in mind that while one or two styles predominate for most people, about fifteen percent use all five styles equally. Those who do are seldom difficult bosses:

> *Synthesists* are creative thinkers who perceive the world in terms of opposites. When you say black, they think white, when you say long, they think short. They are curious (in both senses of the word) people who are interested in anything that doesn't fit a mold. Their conversations are often sprinkled with speculations, "What ifs," and off-the-wall comments that seem little related to the conversations that proceeded them. As they sort through this mishmash of ideas, they often see essential connections that elude more straight-line thinkers, and can thereby produce genuinely new perspectives.
> To connect well with Synthesists, listen appreciatively to

their speculations, and don't confuse their arguing nature with resistance—after all, if you thought in contradictions, you would sound argumentative, too. If you listen to them long enough and are willing to sit through their theorizing, they will often sell themselves on your ideas. Since Synthesist thinkers often see themselves as very clever and creative, it can't help to remind them that you see them that way, too.

Idealists believe in lofty goals and high standards. They ask: Who is benefiting from what we're doing? What are our long-range goals? As managers, they espouse quality, service to others, team work, and cooperation.

Therefore, the more you can associate what you want to do with the goals of quality, service, and community good, the more likely you are to get your Idealist boss's attention. It's equally important not to seem dishonest or untruthful. Not that you can't fool Idealist thinkers—actually they are quite gullible because they deeply believe in the importance of truth. However, once they catch you being devious, they will withdraw their support, often without telling you, and you will find yourself with surface agreement but no action from them.

Idealist-thinking managers strive for agreement, and they feel disappointed and buffaloed when their team can't, won't, or doesn't agree. If you seem unwilling to compromise with others' perspectives, they may be reluctant to grant you full authority.

Pragmatist thinkers are flexible, resourceful folk who look for immediate payoff rather than for a grand plan that will change the world. Pragmatists are not much interested in why things happen, nor in their eventual impact. Thus they tend to tackle problems one step at a time. They are interested in practical, short-term results, and a plan of action that will get things started in the right direction without too much hassle. Pragmatists have a knack for seeing things as they are, especially what others really want, as opposed to what they ought to want, an Idealist preoccupation. Therefore, they are often experts at fitting in and surviving when others fall.

To communicate effectively with Pragmatist-thinking bosses, emphasize short-term objectives on which you can get started with resources at hand. Make sure that they know that you are not ignoring the political aspects of the situation. Don't overwhelm them with a plethora of data or an emphasis on a wonderful overall plan—they'll just get overloaded or bored.

Analyst thinkers equate accuracy, thoroughness, and attention to detail with competence. They like to gather data, measure it, categorize it, and rationally and methodically calculate the right answer to any problem you come up with.

To get the approval of Analyst-thinking bosses you must provide a logical plan replete with back-up data and specifications. Above all, you must *never* submit anything that contains typographical errors, misspelled words, or numbers that do not add up properly. It's not that they'll get angry if you do. It's that they'll dismiss you as anyone competent to be put in charge of anything important.

Realist thinkers are fast-moving doers who *know* that reality is what their senses—sight, sound, taste, smell, and touch—tell them it is, not that dry stuff that one finds in accounting ledgers, or the insipid pages of a manual of operations. As managers, Realists are seldom interested until something goes wrong. Then they move in on the action, get whatever eyewitness testimony there is, and instantly determine what the problem is and what should be done about it. Thankfully, as soon as whatever was broken is once again clinking along, they lose interest in it.

If you communicate with Realist bosses as if they were Analysts, you will never get their attention. Rather than gobs of computer printouts and other detailed information, Realists want a three-paragraph "Executive Summary" which tells *briefly* what is wrong and how you propose to fix it. For rather complicated reasons, they will often take you at your word if they see you as a qualified expert. You become an expert in their eyes when they know that you've assembled a store of facts in which they are interested, *and* you have proposed a set of actions that they already believe are the best things to do.

Certainly people are more complex than these brief sketches imply. Yet it is surprising how much you can avoid rubbing your boss the wrong way by paying close attention to how he or she approaches the tasks of the day. Presenting your ideas in a way that is consonant with your boss's mind is both good sense and highly ethical. Your intention is not to use your boss's natural proclivities against his best interests, but to boost his estimate of your competence so that he will feel more secure in loosening the reins.*

Build Trust by Accepting Fears and Suspicions

Coping successfully with suspicious or fearful bosses will demand more forbearance from you than dealing with the more straightforward nondelegators we've thus far considered. Since you did not cause their fearfulness or chronic suspicion, you are unlikely to cure it, and you certainly do not have the ability to prevent them from projecting it into your work life. There are, however, a number of steps that can widen the range of freedom that they will give you. While none of these steps is particularly difficult, you may find them galling because they call on you to embrace the restrictiveness you hate. However distasteful you may find it, brace yourself and do what your bosses least expect you to do—ask that the reins be temporarily tightened. Be the first to acknowledge that life abounds with inconsistencies and hazards and embrace the wisdom of a cautious and controlled approach. Then, even if the rest of mankind cannot be completely trusted, your boss may find you worthy of more leeway in making decisions. Here are some specifics.

Welcome Frequent Checkups   The more you assure suspicious people, the more they question your sincerity or your good sense. You know that their fears are inordinate, but they don't, so when you insist that all is well, you simply increase their doubts. Paradoxically you can show yourself as a person worthy of trust by welcoming, even insisting on, an even closer look at how well you're doing. If your job requires that you spend money, don't accept a

* For more information about your thinking styles, refer to "The Art of Thinking," in the bibliography, or contact Inq Educational Materials, Inc., P.O. Box 10213, Berkeley, CA 94709, telephone 800-338-2462.

report-back system that merely shows whether you spent the funds for the general purposes for which they were designated. Ask for more, and tighter, controls. If accounts are reconciled monthly, suggest that they be reconciled every two weeks or even weekly because "It's important that we know exactly how that money is being used." It is not important whether or not your slightly paranoid bosses accept your suggestions. It is the fact that you suggested them (without the slight sarcasm that has found its way into my descriptions, naturally) that buttresses their confidence in you. "Ah," you might be thinking, "but what if they accept my proposals? Then, I'm worse off than I was before." While there might be a slight possibility that this will happen, it is much more likely that they will welcome your interest, and then patiently explain that the controls already in existence seem to have been satisfactory. Your object in flowing with the fears of your boss, rather than resisting them, is to mark yourself as "one of those who can be trusted"—a fellow "watcher" who should be granted an increase in responsibility by a grateful boss.

Probe for Clues to Your Boss's Fear Points If you still find reluctance to loosen up, gently probe for the sticking points. You might ask, "What would you need in order to feel secure enough to give me the authority to sign contracts?" Follow up by proposing a *small* and temporary increase in your authority, which both of you will periodically evaluate. Do this even if your boss seems willing to take a larger step. Remember, trust building with a highly suspicious person takes time, and that trust remains fragile even longer.

If Your Boss Equates Mistakes With Failure, Emphasize Contingency Planning Overoptimistic proposals are the rule in most organizations. The competition for funds nudges most competitors for resources to maximize the advantages of their schemes, the ease with which they can be accomplished, and ease of surmounting any hazards that might be encountered en route. For that reason, even seasoned and secure managers learn to anticipate that all will not be as rosy as project developers suggest. When your boss is one who equates minor slipups with disaster and even moderate mistakes with complete catastrophe, it's wise to clearly identify every potential problem before your boss does. Then counterbalance them by emphasizing preventive action. Finally, elaborate on whatever tap dance you've cooked up that will enable your boss to escape if prevention doesn't work. Your purpose is to head off a rush of apprehension that can turn an otherwise bright manager into a hesitant Milquetoast, reluctant to give a go-ahead to any but the tamest of proposals. By openly emphasizing the negative, by clearly showing how you will evade or survive even improbable pitfalls, you provide a safety net, more deeply reassuring than a hundred avowals that all will unfold smoothly.

Provide Verbal Support to Risky Decisions Most people feel less timid when they have company than when alone. You can help some fearful bosses take reasonable chances by emphasizing that "We're all in this together" and by speaking often of "our decision," rather than "your decision." Your hope is that the more supported they feel, the greater the chance that they will trust others—you in particular—to be cautious and therefore relinquish control.

Remind Nervous Bosses That They Really Can Trust You Once this trust-building process has started, you can help it along by frequently affirming your intention to keep both of you out of trouble. Otherwise, your innocent mistake, or an eyebrow raised in your direction from senior management, may provoke suspicion that you have purposely circumvented the safeguards that your boss and you have put into place. Once again, the object of this normally unnecessary rigamarole is to provide a modicum of security to someone with rather shaky self-confidence.

Try Subtle Teaching When you believe you have gained a measure of trust—always assuming that the positive aspects of the job make it worthwhile—suggest, and demonstrate, a less apprehensive view of the world. For example, when something in your own work has gone awry, acknowledge it, but follow up with, "Well, I've learned something from this mistake, here's how I'm going to prevent it in the future." Your goal is to show that there is a way to regard mistakes other than the one currently driving your boss, likely some version of "If I [or someone under my direction] make a mistake it means I've failed, and that is so terrible that I'll never recover from it." While such deeply implanted notions are often discouragingly immune to modification, a few words, spoken by a trusted person, just at the time that events have disproved the truth of that pessimistic dictum, can open the way to a new, more reasonable notion, such as, "Although I don't plan to make mistakes, when they happen, I'm not a failure if I learn from them." In the same vein, you might teach your timid boss that even when mistakes are costly, those costs are usually transitory and, with quick action, can often be contained or minimized. You might say "Well, we [I] may have goofed a little giving advertising first blood to our competitors, *this time*, but now that we know the direction they're taking we're in a better position to counter it." True, that makes a virtue out of a necessity, but not completely. The point you are trying to get across is that while no one chooses to make mistakes, they are seldom the end of the world. Unfortunately the most important step in this process is often the hardest—refrain from denying your own part in any problems that arise. Otherwise you simply reinforce the notion that to be tainted with a mistake is a catastrophe to be avoided at all costs.

5

When Your Boss Must Always Be Right: *The Special Case of Bulldozing Expert Know-It-Alls*

Let's listen to Sally Rider describe her boss:

When Charles interviewed me for this job I was so impressed with him I prayed to get the job. He is an unqualified expert in our line of work, his mind is loaded with practical, well-organized information, he has the confidence and personal strength to put his ideas into action, push them if need be. So why am I trying to get out of this world beater's section? It's simple—he's also turned out to be the world's greatest ass-hole. You want specifics? Well, to start, his brilliant mind closes up like a clam when it's settled on the best approach to take. Once he's decided what's right, he's totally uninflu-encable, a really unstoppable bulldozer. Then, if he thinks I'm not sold 100 percent, he gets in a lecturing mode and goes on and on and on. He's insufferably superior—put quotes around that—condescending and a stuffed shirt, to boot. It's not just that he marks up my reports as if he were the teacher and I were stupid pupil, what burns me is that he doesn't simply make the changes himself, he leaves little notes telling me exactly what to do. Some of what he wants is just a matter of style, a lot is completely trivial—I'd used a comma instead of a semi-colon—and, sure, a few are really

87

well taken. What really scares me is that lately I've found myself sending in the absolute minimum I can get by with. Let him fill in the blanks first, and then I'll do the report. It saves me time and it doesn't give him the satisfaction of feeling that he's always smart and I'm always dumb.

Charles is the kind of Difficult Boss I call the Expert Know-It-All. While, in truth, their "I'm always right" attitude is a constant irritation, that is not what boosts them to the front rank of Difficult Bosses. It is their knack for pulling incompetent behavior out of able subordinates like Sally.

These heavyweights of fact and reason are described by their subordinates as unstoppable, unfazable, and uncaring, sufficient reason to call them by the name given to their mechanical brethren—Bulldozers. For example, they always have the right answer to every question, not *a* right answer, *the* right answer. When anyone disagrees, they react as if it were a personal contradiction rather than a simple difference of opinion, cutting off the conversation in an obvious huff. Bulldozers are, indeed, often accused of acting in a very "superior" manner, spurning others' ideas as if they were the thoughts of befuddled children. And why should they not, for they are certain that their plans and ideas *are* better than any others. They equate accuracy and throughness with competence, are unforgiving of minor errors, and tend to have little understanding or patience with the irrational aspects of human behavior such as feelings, wishes, and intuitions. Because they are knowledgeable, and because they thoroughly research and carefully plan everything they do, they often leave their less-linear-thinking subordinates feeling vaguely inadequate. In fact, the most frustrating aspect of reporting to an Expert Know-It-All is that 75 percent of the time, he or she will turn out to be correct. Sadly, as it did with Sally, a Bulldozer's overweening manner—pompous, patronizing, and pontifical—often calls up memories of impatient parents, who always knew better, and otherwise able employees find themselves drawn into a childlike subterranean rebellion. They show their "independence" by refusing to give fully of their abilities, in a sense "flaunting" their incompetence. Thus the strange circle is completed and the Know-It-All's perception of the inadequacy of most of the rest of mankind is substantiated. It is not hard to see why they are reluctant to trust others with any but the most routine or menial tasks.

Understanding Expert Know-It-Alls

Recall the characteristics of the Analyst thinkers we touched upon in chapter 4. They are solid, methodical thinkers who value data and a logical approach to everything, without doubt a valuable and productive way to handle a sometimes capricious world.

But take that Analyst thinker, teach her that careful calculation is the only proper way to solve problems, add to that exacting mind a heavy dose of aggressiveness and a wish to be like those powerful know-it-all parents, and you have a recipe for a stubborn, self-righteous fountain of knowledge—the bulldozing Expert Know-It-All.

Of all of the Difficult Bosses I've studied, Expert Know-It-Alls are the hardest to influence. I suspect that the knowledge of their own competence, plus the frequent lapses into resistant sloppiness of their subordinates, leads them to the conviction that they are the standard to which all human beings should aspire. From that lofty perspective, one does not often pay heed to the gibberings of inferiors. It is certainly not impossible to get a Bulldozer's attention, but to do so may require more effort and persistence than you wish to invest.

One option is to quit. That decision should rest on a straightforward cost/benefit analysis, which gives weight to the toll your boss is taking on your self-efficacy. Another option is to reaffirm to yourself that you are not the difficult person, your boss is. Having done that, having stopped wishing that he or she were different, you will be in a position to choose to work for such a boss because, pain in the rear or not, this is a treasure house of knowledge from whom you can learn much. Having so chosen, there are a number of ploys that will help to lessen the degree to which you feel belittled, and, at times, may dramatically turn the situation around.

Coping With Expert Know-It-Alls

To cope with Bulldozers, you need to demonstrate your own competence in a fashion that does not challenge their standing as "experts."

Prepare as Well as You Can   Since Expert Know-It-Alls are harsher critics of incomplete, slipshod, or carelessly assembled work than most other bosses, an absolute precursor to coping effectively with one of these worthies is careful preparation of any assignments. To put it plainly, you must always do your homework. Did you hate to prepare alphabetized term-paper outlines for your eleventh-grade teacher, and even now prefer getting into action to step-by-step planning? Nonetheless, if you report to a Bulldozer, force yourself to methodically plan each of your projects, replete with the background data—preferably in tabular form—and an analysis, slathered with concrete details, of precisely what is to be done, and how much it will cost. If you are asked for recommendations, stick to yes or no responses, never "maybe," and document your reasons for either answer. Proofread anything in print, including inconsequential memos, for typographical errors, misspelled words, and especially incorrect calculations. They are to be avoided, not merely minimized. Don't expect kudos for having taken these pains—after all, you are only behaving as any sound-thinking person should. What you *can* expect, however, is that you will move from the "careless troublemaker" category in your boss's mind to the "okay" category. Without that relabeling, other coping efforts will have little effect.

Work for Limited Delegation Goals   Since Expert Know-It-Alls tend to be cautious by nature, it's wise to suggest that any freedom to act on your own be confined to a limited area. If possible, choose tasks with easily measurable results, not of any personal interest to your boss. For example, if you manage the home-improvement section in a department store and your Bulldozing supervisor is an expert in paints, varnishes, and other wall coverings, propose that, on a trial basis, you be permitted to make the final ordering and pricing decisions for small appliances. You chose small appliances because your boss seemed to consider it an unimportant profit center, at least as compared to wall coverings, and also because you have taken pains to make yourself an expert by thoroughly digesting every appliance catalogue around.

Don't Fight Their Expertise   Bulldozers are proud of their expertise and expect it to be recognized and valued by others. Since they *are* experts, at least in certain areas, showing respect for their knowledge, while perhaps it may not help much, certainly can't hurt. Feeding a large ego in a way that is legitimate can lessen its need to gobble every scrap of the credit that ought to be spread around to others.

Use Questions to Point Out Problems   Directly disputing your boss's conclusions is likely to provoke argument rather than agreement. So what course is open to you when you believe his plan, "completely logical" or not, won't work? Perhaps some vital fact was dismissed because it couldn't be stuffed into a rational category, or a vagary of public opinion was not taken seriously. While you see the flaw clearly, how do you bring it into focus, without provoking a defensive, stonewalling reaction? In that fix, your best tactics are two special kinds of questions, designed to lead your boss into discovering his own mental lapse before, rather than after, disaster befalls. I call them "Baby Blue Eyes" and "Extensional" questions.

Baby Blue Eyes questions always end with "Can (could) you explain that to me?" For example, "I don't exactly see how your marketing plan will put us ahead of our competitors, Mr. Smith, can you explain that to me," or, "Our problem has been that our line managers simply don't read the administrative manual, Ms. Jones, could you explain that to me?" Having posed those naïve questions, you bat your baby blues and look innocent while your boss "explains" it all (regrettably often at great length).

An Extensional question simply asks another to extend his or her ideas or plans over time or space. For example, you might say, "I think I understand your plan for improving our performance review process, Tom. Now could you describe just how that will work in each of our seven divisions since they are all a little different."

You gain in several ways from raising such questions. First, your boss might indeed be able to show you that your concerns were without foundation. By questioning rather than confronting you save yourself embarrassment and avoid adding to your boss's certainty that you're an idiot. Second, you will be drawing on the undoubted strengths of Expert Know-It-Alls. Aren't they, much more than others, swayed by facts and logic, especially their *own* facts and logic. While she recapitulates each brick in the grand edifice, you hope your boss will suddenly see the logic gaps, misjudgments, or overlooked contingencies. Why now and not before? Because you posed questions that asked for description, not defense or justification.

Help Your Boss Save Face   Suppose none of this works. Your expert boss, obdurate to the end, insists on steadfastly chugging out of the areas in which he or she is knowledgeable into calamity. There may be no alternative but directly pointing out faulty facts or conclusions. When you must so beard the lion, you will boost the odds of being taken seriously *and* minimize angry repercussions, if you cushion your boss's ego with a face-saving rationalization. True, it might be wonderfully satisfying to shout, "See, see," while gleefully showing your boss how badly the budget figures were misquoted at yesterday's meeting. There is an almost irresistible siren call to gleefully help an always-right boss stumble. As enticing as that might be, I suggest that you resist. For, when their carefully wrought programs do go awry, Bulldozers blame others for the disaster. Because you may have had a hand in implementing the plan, *and*, even more to the point, you're near at hand, the accusing finger may point directly at you, an outcome you would prefer to avoid.

Instead, wonder out loud to your boss if she or he "weren't probably thinking of the budget of the year before," or "the tentative budget we talked about for awhile," or even, "I may have confused you with some of the questions I was asking." Your purpose in this charade is not to coddle your boss, but to avoid angry retorts or vindictive behavior, a Bulldozer's two favorite responses to those who have been defined as an enemy.

There May Be a Bonus While it's true that coping with Expert Bulldozers may require more persistence than you would like to invest, it is often worth it. Benefits can range from less heavyhanded control over limited areas of your job, to an almost complete turn-around, when your Expert Know-It-All comes to see you as an expert in your own right. You will have engineered this little miracle yourself by doing your homework, by openly recognizing the knowledgeability and worth of an undoubted expert, and by raising well-thought-out and pertinent questions that unobtrusively clarified weighty matters. True, you may never be accorded status as a first-class expert—is there ever room for more than one of those in any unit?—but even second-class experts deserve privileges. Suddenly you will find that your boss is willing to expand the area in which you have complete—well, to be realistic, mostly complete—authority, and your comments will be sought *before* the final plans have been set. Perhaps you will be invited along to meetings formerly exclusively attended by the only person whose brain really counted, your boss. You will know that you have attained this state of grace when you are coopted into lamenting with your boss about all of the mental midgets you both must endure. At that point there may be nothing left to do but nod your head and smile knowingly.

When Your Boss Is Unscrupulous or Offensive: *Scalawags, Schemers, and Skunks*

In a sense, the Difficult Bosses we've examined in the preceding chapters are as much victims of their mental and emotional makeups as are their much abused subordinates. While much of their behavior may be objectionable in the extreme, their intentions, like ours, are to fulfill their organizational commitments and to otherwise advance the enterprise. In this chapter, however, we'll take on a genuinely distasteful trio of bosses whose intentions are largely self-serving, unscrupulous, or offensive. They violate our sense of decency, they operate with sneak and stealth, and they leave behind a malodorous and unhealthful aura. What better labels for the three varieties most commonly found in the workplace than Scalawags, Schemers, and Skunks. Scalawags prey on others for their own self-gain, taking credit for work that was not their own or using their power to extort money or favors from others. Schemers are out for their own gain with little thought to the costs of their behavior to the enterprise, or to the community in which they work. Skunks knowingly offend others and in other ways figuratively stink up the atmosphere.

The Behavior

The following brief descriptions, drawn from my client notes, not only illustrate the unsavory behavior of all three but also point up the repugnant choices facing those unlucky enough to work for them.

* Gena, a bookkeeper in the customer-service unit of a large appliance store:
    Sylvia [the service manager] made me add 20 percent to each invoice so she could show a profit for the Service Center. When customers would complain—it's funny, but only a handful ever did—she would blame it on "a bookkeeping error," which made me look bad. This went on for over three years until she was promoted. I never dared to tell her that I thought it was dishonest, so I never told anyone else.
* Ben, a supervising electronics technician in a large high-tech manufacturing firm:
    My old boss, Rodney Belson, regularly sent pieces of my weekly reports up to headquarters under his name. Since they included some pretty good suggestions for redesigning parts to save on scrap and get better yields, he got rave notices and I got nothing. Finally, when he was given, and took, a "bright idea bonus" of five hundred dollars for one of my ideas, I blew the whistle on him. I had nothing in writing, and he lied about it, of course, so they believed him instead of me. Afterward, he spread the word that I was a troublemaker and I think he would have tried to fire me if he could have gotten away with it. It was a really bad time for me, and I quit soon afterward anyway. I not only lost my seniority and pension contribution, but then that shit wouldn't even give me a decent reference. Sure, I got another job, but the big problem was that I felt I couldn't trust anyone. That went on for a long time.

- Marianne, human-resources director for a state agency in the Midwest:

  You want to know what the problems are that we have in this department? [Here Marianne paused to query me on the confidentiality of our interview.] Well, I guess I can trust you. The biggest problem is our esteemed director, Mr. Santos. In a nutshell, he lies about everything to everyone, and he uses our hard-to-get tax dollars to feather his own political nest. Oh, he's pretty slick about it. For example, last year he gave grants to a bunch of not very deserving community organizations run by friends who had lobbied for him being appointed to this job. He's kept the lid on some very hot problems so that he and his pal in the State House could look good before the election. It's against the rules, but, twice, he's put the arm on all of us execs to come up with campaign contributions by giving a big party at his house and then asking us right there to drop money in a hat. He didn't even pass the hat around so some could get away without putting anything in. We had to walk up to the front of the room and put some paper in. As far as I'm concerned he's a crook, but what can I do? I'm a twenty-year civil servant who's supposed to follow the orders of the elected officials and their appointed agency heads. I used to love this job. Now I hate everything about it.

- Olivia, a secretary in a brokerage office:

  Mr. Jarvis is simply an asshole. He comes on to all the females, or at least the young ones; he calls us "babe" or "cookie," he—oh, I know it all sounds stupid and silly for me to be so sure about it, but it's his whole attitude. I asked him not to call me "babe," but he just told me it was his way and if I didn't like it I could quit. My problem is—I know this sounds terrible—but the pay and benefits are so good here, I don't want to give them up. Of course he knows that, and that's why he feels free.

- Don, R & D manager for a medium-size manufacturing company:

  Dr. Bramson, have I got a story for you! In fact, I've been waiting all week to tell you about it. George Crawford, our vice president for sales—or so he was until two weeks ago—was finally caught with his hand in the till. Starting about two years ago, he began changing his regional managers' sales forecasts upward and making them sign off on them. Then, to come through on those inflated forecasts, and get the hefty bonus that went along, he shipped product to customers who hadn't ordered it. When the stuff was sent back weeks later, it didn't show up on the balance sheet as a missed sale, but as a return. I don't know how he thought he could get away with it, but he actually did for quite a while. Maybe it would have gone on forever, but finally two junior people on the sales staff, both women by the way, complained to the CEO, and George was fired. Guess who the new VP for sales is? One of the regional managers who had the good sense—sorry for the sarcasm— to keep his mouth shut about Crawford's shenanigans.

To keep the classification scheme straight, Rodney Belson and Director Santini seem eminently skilled as Scalawags, Sylvia and George Crawford fill the bill as Schemers, and by most criteria Mr. Jarvis suitably qualifies as a Skunk.

Understanding Unscrupulous and Offensive Bosses

While our understanding of the basis of evil is certainly incomplete, most authorities concur that three inner forces, alone or in combination, are the source of most malevolent behavior: an aberrant set of values, a fear—realistic or fantasied—of the very people whom they victimize, and an eerie inability to feel for, and with, others. As you read further, keep in mind that the goal is neither justification nor forgiveness, but understanding.

An Aberrant Set of Values   To a considerable extent what we value directs our behavior, that of Schemers, Skunks, and Scalawags included. It's the nature of their values, not the lack of them, that sets them apart. As repellent as that sort of "morality" may feel, none of us did much choosing of the values inculcated in us when we were young, so even these victimizers are victims themselves. Although you may never fully understand how *anyone* could act that way, some people do believe that it is clever to steal from others, that it's astute to abuse others to get what you want, and that those who let themselves be so cheated or abused deserve it. No wonder they are so infuriatingly pleased with themselves for conforming admirably to a set of bent standards. Therefore, when your reprehensible coworkers do not heed your admonitions to behave in a proper manner, remind yourself that to their own lights they are. Sadly they are often reinforced in their beliefs by the admiration of others. For example, ruthlessness can masquerade as strength and quickness of mind; thus it paradoxically repels and fascinates, especially in times of personal, social, or organizational disruption. It's not by accident that dictatorships and dictatorial bosses come to power when times are shaky.

Fear While it is often masked by bravado, many victimizers are genuinely, if irrationally, fearful of their victims. "If we don't get 'them,' 'they'll' get us," captures the main thrust of the feeling. You can substitute for "them" and "they," "women," "blacks," "Jews," "Asians," "the unions," "the brass," or any other group of which the victimizer is not a member.

As with any other difficult behavior, attacking feared "others' has its own satisfactions, convoluted as they may be. For example, if scoundrels succeed in hurting you in some way, they prove themselves to be powerful and capable of conquering an enemy that they fear. If they attack you and lose, they have demonstrated the soundness of their fear and can console themselves with "just you wait till next time."

Inability to Feel for Others Some people routinely harm others without seeming to care too much about it. Although

Similarly, some insensitive souls can bumble themselves into ethical problems simply because they are unware of the full consequences of what they are doing. Lacey Thomas, a capable management consultant, found herself becoming increasingly irritated by a manager who, in the presence of others, insisted on calling her "honey," "sweetheart," or "doll." At length she said to him, privately, "I need to tell you that my name is Lacey, and I would appreciate it if you would use my name when you're speaking to me." Although he claimed that it was simply his way of talking to people, from that point on, with only an occasional lapse, he stopped. Later, Lacey heard, with no little delight, that he had asked every other woman in his work group, "Does it really bother you that I don't use your name?" He was shocked at the number of yeses he heard.

To distinguish these gnats—irritating but seldom really harmful—from truly objectionable bosses, two rather straightforward techniques will usually suffice.

First, as Lacey discovered, matter-of-fact honesty will often be enough to turn the unwitting offenders to more acceptable behavior. Your emphasis should be as positive as possible, that is, state what you want from them rather than focusing on what they're doing that you don't like. In that way you minimize the possibility that they'll respond defensively. Lacey's "I would appreciate it if . . ." is an example. If your honesty generates a sniping retort such as "You're just too sensitive," or "Can't you take a joke?" be ready to respond with a restatement of what you expect, a solid and assertive counter to such disguised attacks—"However you meant it, from now on I expect you to use my name when you refer to me." It often helps to give your boss a face-saving way out by inserting a phrase such as "I expect you didn't know that it bothered me" at an appropriate place in the conversation. Keep in mind that your purpose is to stop disagreeable behavior, not punish or insult.

Similarly, if your boss is lying a little—exaggerating projected sales, or understating potential losses—a few words such as "I'm sure a lot of other people may do it around here, boss, but I worry about it" ("am uncomfortable doing it") should suffice. They may not move your boss to follow the rules, but at least they should get you out of the rule-bending loop.

If neither of these approaches works, assume that your boss is indeed a shifty double-dealer and move on to the next coping steps.

Clarify What You're Up Against Before taking action, it's vital that you determine as well as you can just what you're up against—you'll want no surprises—what your own goals are, and how you want it all to work out. Thinking through these questions will help:

- Is your boss's behavior illegal or simply unethical? While both may be reprehensible to you, illegality has consequences (fines or jail sentences) not present when immorality is the only issue. Have you been co-opted into becoming a party to illegal schemes? What is the extent of your involvement? Have you been forced to participate in or actively condone illegal activities, or are you just silently looking the other way? Unfair as it may seem, in the eyes of the law, Gena, the bookkeeper in our early example, who went along with her boss Sylvia's unearned "surcharge" scheme, would to some extent share Sylvia's guilt, even though Gena internally decried such dishonesty.

- Do others in your work group share your perception that something is awry? Do you believe so because they spontaneously make comments or do they only assent to yours? Remember that coworkers will often passively agree with vehemently stated opinions, just be polite or to avoid hassles.

- Is there support from above for the nefarious behavior being forced upon you, or is your boss acting alone? Is that support open, covert, or the incidental result of poor review or control procedures? Some clues: Is there a section in the employee manual on business ethics; is there a published "whistle-blowing" phone number; how do human-resources staff react when you discuss your problem with them—for example, do they excuse it, attempt to shrug it off, or give attention and follow it up with action?

- What are your own goals? How repellent is the unethical behavior to you? Are you offended because what is happening is truly wrong, or is it just that you don't want to be involved? What are the one or two most important things you'd like to see changed? What is your bottom line, that is, under what circumstances will you feel obligated to disconnect yourself from this boss, this unit, this organization?

- What are the likely costs if you take action, or if you do not? When considering the latter, keep in mind that most people who violate their own (not necessarily society's, or anyone else's) deeply felt standards of behavior will eventually make amends by getting themselves caught, becoming sick, anxious, or depressed.

Having made your assessment, you're ready to choose the most appropriate coping steps to include in your action plan.*

Disengage, if Practicable

Because coping with unscrupulous or offensive bosses is unpleasant work, removing yourself from the unsavory situation is often a tempting alternative. It also may be the best one. Here are some questions that can help you decide:

- Do you feel morally bound to try to change the situation? Keep in mind that working to bring about desirable changes does not necessarily mean acerbic confrontations. Persistent, low-level resistance can, over time, make a difference.

- What are the potential costs to you if you don't disengage? Consider the state of your conscience, possible legal liability, and your potential for promotion in an organization with values antithetical to your own.

* In chapter 8 you'll find a more thorough discussion of the value of planning before coping with a Difficult Boss.

- Do you have a practicable alternative? Can you transfer to another unit within the organization? What's the current job market for a person with your background and skills? To what extent is a lower-paying position preferable to living with fear or distaste?

Sometimes you can have greater impact by resigning and making public the reasons for your departure. Senior executives who have previously excused borderline behavior in their subordinate managers often take a closer look when they find that competent employees are leaving. Similarly you may find it less personally arduous to bring culprits to justice when you are no longer a part of the organization. If you decide to resign before taking action, be sure to keep handy any and all records of your own achievements, commendations, and positive performance reviews. Unhappily the first, and too often successful, defense against the accusations of former employees is that they were discharged or "allowed to resign" for poor performance, and that they are simply being vindictive.

If You Decide to Stick Around, Take Care of Yourself

Are you an employee caught in a situation similar to one of the examples cited at the beginning of this chapter? Have you been ordered by your boss to take part in skulduggery, been subjected to humiliation because of your sex, race, or other personal characteristic, been a witness to political manipulation, or been forced to stand by while a lying boss takes credit for your best ideas? Are there good reasons that prevent you from simply moving out of the morass? If so, do something, anything, to insulate yourself from the unhealthy conditions around you. No matter how minimal, positive action will lessen those illness-producing feelings of helpless anger that I've mentioned in previous chapters. Here are some action suggestions that will help keep you on an even emotional keel.

Resist   Do everything you safely can to covertly jam the works. To the extent possible, be as inefficient as you can without jeopardizing your position. Accidentally misplace papers, overrun deadlines, and in other ways throw a few grains of sand in the organizational gearbox. Such minor-league foot dragging can serve two beneficial purposes. First, it can boost your morale. Even prisoners in the worst of concentration-camp environments have described the elation that they felt from hiding crumbs of food to be given to weaker compatriots, or allowing machinery to malfunction from a lack of proper lubrication. Second, if you and your like-minded colleagues are inefficient enough, and cost overruns accumulate, outside investigators may descend and curb the activities of which you disapprove.

Write Down and Talk About Your Feelings   When you are forced to violate your personal credo you can expect a serious confusion of emotions—anger, fear, disgust—with both your bosses and yourself. You may begin to doubt the rightness of your own values, wondering if you are not in truth too naïve to accept the reality that whatever wins has got to be right. To avoid this sense of ethical imbalance, capture your feelings on paper and, if feasible, talk them over with someone you trust. Don't worry about literary merit, or the reasonableness of what you're thinking and feeling. Pour what's inside you onto the paper as fully as possible. "I was really angry," is no substitute for "I could have strangled that scum for bragging about my idea as if it was his own." What you're striving for is the temporary relief and perspective that invariably comes when you transform a jumbled mess of confused feelings into words and sentences.

Similarly, talking over your nasty situation with valued friends or family members can serve an important purpose. As you tell your story, you may find yourself reevaluating whether you can, should, or wish to remain in circumstances that are taking such a toll on you. Further, if you detect reluctance to reveal the part you're playing in potentially dishonest or unethical goings-on, take that hesitancy as a not-to-be-denied signal that the costs of remaining in the situation may be too great. Janie, office manager for a large dental practice, and single mother, had exactly that experience.

When Janie discovered that the dentist owner of the practice had instructed the bookkeeper—nominally under her charge—to invoice government agencies and insurance companies for procedures more elaborate than those that were carried out, she was somewhat troubled. However, wanting to keep her job, she did nothing. After all, she told herself, according to the luncheon grapevine, several other dentists in the area were profiting from this sort of illegal billing. At length, after she was offered a cut of the illegal profits, she discussed the situation with her teenage daughter. Her daughter's appalled reaction convinced Janie that she needed to resign her position, and she did. When later I asked her whether she had then reported the dentist-owner's illegal practices to the authorities, she said that she had not. When she had resigned he had pointedly told her that "if he went down he would take the rest of the staff with him," and that meant several coworkers that she had come to regard as real friends. When I suggested that her friends could have made the same choice she did, she smiled, perhaps a little ruefully, and said, "They might not be 'lucky' enough to have such a puritanical daughter."

Consider Counseling   Most of us, when mired in a seemingly impossible quandary, become so emotionally overloaded that, just when we need the clearest of minds, we find it difficult to think rationally about what to do. Therefore, consider scheduling some visits with a professional counselor. That's especially wise if other talking-out possibilities are not available to you; for example, you may be a single parent of very young children, new in the area and without close friends. Laying out your problem to a paid "friend," whose confidentiality can be assumed, can help you sort out both your feelings and the alternatives realistically open to you.

Document, Document, Document

The moment you suspect that your boss is violating the rules of proper behavior, start collecting evidence. If you receive a signed note from your boss asking you to cook the books or to refrain from hiring someone because of race, creed, national origin, disability, sex, or age, copy it and keep it in your lock box. If you are not fortunate enough to have that sort of clear documentation (and stupid boss), make careful, dated notes that described every objectionable thing you are asked, or ordered, to do.

Equally important, record what you have done in response, including protests made, when, to whom, and in what form. Where possible, make verbatim notes or tape record conversations that you suspect just might be troublesome later. Keep your documentation in a personal file, and not in the office. (I know of several instances in which employees were summarily fired and escorted off the premises with no opportunity to collect personal belongings.) Consider sealing a copy or two of damaging notes in an envelope, dating it, and asking a creditable witness to hold it for you. While none of these steps will *prove* that you were not an active party to the shenanigans, they are convincing evidence that you were concerned, that you took appropriate steps to notify others, and that you did not voluntarily participate in the illegal activities.

You may find that you're feeling sneaky and underhanded about taking such precautions. Counter that feeling with the knowledge that the kinds of bosses we're dealing with in this chapter will not ever protect you; you will have to do that for yourself. Well-intentioned people working in an ethically unhealthy environment sometimes believe that they can sustain themselves by doing their own jobs honestly and well and thus remain untainted by what is happening around them. Only when they find themselves protesting their innocence on a witness stand do they realize that their actions might lend themselves to a less-than-innocent interpretation. It was that fateful reality that Arnold Sacco, thirty-two-year-old head of the regional service center for a major supplier of medical instruments, discovered, when confronted by his signature on incriminating documents. Catastrophically, for him, it was the only signature.

As a regional manager, Arnold approved the service contracts and pricing arrangements negotiated by his regional salespeople. Occasionally, however, very large service and supply contracts were negotiated solely by the senior manager to whom he reported. He was neither surprised nor concerned when the contracts were then sent to him for his signature, since the work would eventually come under his supervision. While Arnold did wonder about the high prices approved by some customers, often much higher than his salesmen were able to obtain, he was assured by his boss that the customers were aware of what they were doing, and were willing to go along for their own reasons. However, six months later a major government agency complained to the local district attorney about price gouging by Arnold's company. Arnold's boss vehemently denied that he had anything to do with such gross profiteering and his denials were backed up by the purchasing agents in the complaining agency. Arnold suddenly found that is was he who was charged with fraud. While Arnold was certain that he had been caught in the middle of a collusive arrangement between his boss and those same purchasing people, he could not prove it. To the contrary, there was his signature on each of those contracts. Yes, he knew that the pricing arrangements were out of line, and he had questioned them. But his superiors could remember no such conversations, and he could not state in any detail when and where they had occurred. Although some of the senior executives in his company privately wondered about what had really happened, they weren't willing to risk the reputation of the company by inquiring too closely. Nor was the district attorney that enamored of trading a sure conviction for the slim possibility that taking on Arnold's company would pay political dividends. To mount a full-scale investigation of his own would have bankrupted Arnold, so when he was offered a chance to plead guilty in return for probation, he did so. Thankfully he was able to find a job, at a hierarchical notch lower, to be sure, in a distantly located company. It is a sad comment on our public morality that his new employers, told in detail about what had happened, completely believed his story. They evidently did not find his woeful tale too much out of the ordinary.

As Arnold painfully discovered, great performance reviews and good intentions may not be enough protection. Especially when large sums of money are involved, you'll need to be wary, and document, document, document.

If You Must Bring Charges

At times you may find yourself forced, by your own ethical standards or by a need to protect yourself, into that arduous and often thankless task euphemistically known as "blowing the whistle." Making nefarious activities public is often an uphill battle for reasons that are understandable if not laudable. If it is your own boss you are accusing, it is unlikely that he or she will cooperate in the investigation and, senior executives, whether or not they plan to remedy the situation later, may move disconcertingly slowly, if, indeed, they move. Those in charge often take as their first responsibility ensuring their organization's survival and growth. Neither of those objectives are advanced when illegal or unethical activities become public. Unfortunately it's almost always easier for an organization to get rid of the problem by getting rid of the employee, than to reform the lack of controls or implicit sanctions that allowed the unsatisfactory conditions to arise. Ruth Perkins, an attractive woman in her middle thirties, who had been referred to me by her attorney, described such an experience.

> Jim Arnold and I—he was chief buyer then and I was an associate buyer—had had dinner together a few times—neither of us was married and it seemed okay. Well, a year ago, out of the blue, he suggested that we share a room at an industry convention "to save money." When I refused, he became furious and threatened to fire me for being uncooperative. I told him that I would have no compunction about telling his boss, a senior VP, about what happened, but I

suggested that we both simply forget about it and go back to working together as we had before.

Since that time, my job has been in shambles. My office was taken away, I've been downgraded to assistant buyer, and my last performance review stunk. I've talked to everyone in the hierarchy I can think of and all I've gotten is bullshit. They say their hands are tied because Arnold denies everything, and they have no proof. They also claim that my demotion was part of a general budget crunch, and that they don't see how they can make him change my performance review because "there are no fixed standards for what makes a good buyer." My lawyer says if I sue I might be able to get a "nuisance settlement" just by threatening to file, but then what? Sometimes I think I should just forget it and hope things will get better over time. The problem is that right now I'm so sore about this I can hardly think of anything else. The fact is that it really is affecting how well I'm doing my job.

At the point Ruth and I began to work together, the only reasonable focus for our consultations was giving her some relief from her emotional overload and helping her regain the ability to make some rational choices. For her, the best choice was to disengage herself as best she could and rebuild her faltering sense of self-worth. Some of Ruth's frustration, of course, could have been avoided if she had taken a few of the steps we've already touched upon, assessing the situation before she acted, documenting everything that had happened, and checking with others to see whether they'd had the same or similar experiences. Yet even those steps may not have been enough, given the inequality of numbers and power that are the reality when employee takes on organization. Here are several "equalizing" actions that may just be enough to keep you safe when you can't keep silent.

Try for Collective Security   Do your best to engage your colleagues in a joint whistle-blowing undertaking. For one thing, it will be more difficult for others to doubt your credibility or take vindictive action against you, if more than one of you is alleging wrongdoing. At least you'll know that if your complaint gets serious attention, you'll have witnesses to call on. Marianne Tillman, the human-resources director whose boss Mr. Santos had engaged in political skulduggery, privately shared her increasing frustration about Santos with a few coworkers she trusted the most. She found two who also suspected that he was subverting accepted community grant procedures to reward politically active favorites. Although she failed to persuade either of them to commit their suspicions to writing, she did obtain promises of support should she take action. (When she mentioned this to me, I felt bound to point out that private assurances of public support can only be cautiously counted on. This is especially true when tongues have been lubricated by alcohol, or the warm, companionable feelings that accompany an after-hours complaining session.) Still, knowing that she was not the only one who had taken offense was supportive in itself, and believing that she had company enabled her to take the next step. We'll get to that shortly.

Attack the Problem, Not the Person   Even responsible executives are reluctant to accuse a subordinate manager with whom they've had years of a friendly relationship. However, they are usually quite willing to institute measures designed to correct an organizational "systems problem." By accusing the system, rather than the person, you improve your chances of closing down the offensive activities. To achieve one goal—stopping the sleazy machinations, you may have to give up on another—seeing the rat properly stomped. Examples of this approach are:

- Note in suggestion box (assuming it's ever opened): "It might encourage creativity if employees could send their 'bright idea bonus' suggestions directly to the human-resources office without having to get their boss's okay."
- Memo or "chance" remark to corporate controller: "It appears to me from my position as a district office bookkeeper that a random comparison of service-call invoices with employee time cards might be a useful safeguard."

- Memo to training department: "I've had some experiences that lead me to believe that additional training for managers on eliminating sexism (racism, age discrimination . . .) in our organization would be worthwhile."

To be sure, such proposals might just provoke further inquiries, to which you will respond matter-of-factly by describing why you believe that the changes you proposed are necessary, with documentation if requested. Try to remain a problem-solver, rather than an accuser, at least until those inquiring have voiced their own concerns that your boss is out of line. Why is this approach effective? My hunch is that your stance as a problem-solver puts you on the side of the organization, at least in the eyes of those with power to change things. You are not a troublemaker. Just a good citizen after the same goal of proper conduct that the organizational standard-bearers say they want. At least it increases your chances of being supported rather than placated, ostracized, or attacked. At any rate, it worked reasonably well for Marianne Tillman when she finally took action against department director Santos. It happened this way. During one of her frequent visits to the state capitol she set up lunch with one of the governor's middle-level staff members whom she knew from a previous assignment. Over coffee, she wondered—out loud—whether she was right in assuming that while the governor might value the support of local community leaders, he would want to avoid a potential scandal over the award of community grant funds outside of the standard review and priority-setting system. When her companion asked for specifics, she provided them, pointing out that while Mr. Santos had indeed ordered that the grants be made without a "complete review," she thought that he might not be fully aware of the rules. She was frank in saying that she had been most reluctant to make too much of it because she knew how important those local people were to the governor. Although Santos was never formally disciplined by the governor's office—much to Marianne's relief since it allowed her to remain a silent player, she found the net result was satisfactory. Shortly after her conversation with the governor's man, a formal note was circulated among all agency directors reminding them that no funds could be allocated to local organizations without complying with the letter of standard review procedures. Santos was furious, her first happy event, said Marianne, since he had taken over two years previously. Six months later, she called again, unsuccessfully trying to keep a certain elation out of her voice, to tell me—in case I had not read about it in the newspapers—that upon his reelection the governor had not reappointed Santos.

Coping with people who lack scruples is a complicated affair. It's easy to feel immobilized just by the difficulty of knowing what isn't acceptable behavior these days. When friendly (at least in their television commercials) corporations take advantage of unsettled world conditions to raise prices, might not a little personal gouging be no more than fair? Doesn't the prize indeed belong to the quickest, and, if so, isn't padding invoices just a tiny bit worse? Less apparent, but no less troublesome, is ambivalence about who's to blame. Some good souls, realizing that all of us, bad and good, are equal victims of our genes and life experiences, "make allowances," hint and hope that wrongdoers will see the light or will receive their rewards in heaven.

At such times, the only dependable litmus test of proper behavior is what your own deeply held convictions say it is. If you find yourself swept into activities that you believe are wrong, take some active steps to cope, no matter how small. That may be all that you need do to survive, and even learn from the experience. As Michael Lombardo of the Center for Leadership Studies in North Carolina has pointed out, most successful people have survived and even benefited from encounters with noxious bosses. They gained inner strength, they learned what not to do when themselves in positions of power, and, as a kind of bonus for hazardous duty, they often earned considerable credit from others for coping effectively with their Schemers, Scalawags, and Skunks.

7

When a Sweet Boss Turns Sour: *Coping With Crossed Expectations, Behavior Blindness, and Interactional Accidents*

So far, our attention has been on an assortment of bad guys. While they may not always intend to do you in, their personality or character flaws, magnified by the power of their positions, have turned them into truly Difficult Bosses. Luckily they are relatively few in number. My estimate is that fewer than 20 percent of all of the bosses that you will encounter in your career can fairly be placed in this "bad boss" category. Unfortunately it is not only these clearly irksome fellows who contribute to boss-related anguish. Nice, normal people, not too different from yourselves, can look, sound, and feel like Difficult Bosses when the circumstances are right. In this chapter we'll examine the most common of these circumstances: crossed expectations, behavior blindness, and interactional accidents. Then we'll describe the coping steps that can nudge these transient bad guys back into the "good guy" column.

Crossed Expectations

A host of excellent organizational studies have shown that managers and those they manage usually have widely different notions about their respective roles, and especially about how much and what kind of authority was handed over along with the tasks that have been delegated. In consequence both manager and managed proceed to disappoint each other by not fulfilling the other's expectations. For example, Jill, a human-resources director, may say to Jack, a senior personnel technician, "You are now in charge of employee interviewing." Jack, elated by an interesting new assignment, develops new selection standards, revises interview protocols and improves procedures for referring acceptable candidates to the supervisors for whom they will work. Jack's elation will quickly turn to resentment, however, when Jill not only objects to certain features of these new arrangements, but blithely assumes that as the boss it is her word that should prevail. To annoyed Jack, the delegation was meaningless—"The director still wants to make all of the important decisions." Director Jill's version will typically be quite different. "When I told Jack that he was in charge of interviewing, I meant that it was his job to see that everything ran smoothly, and he'd have the final say as to whether an applicant is suitable for our company. Naturally I expect to review any changes in policies and procedures. It puzzles me that a good person like Jack should be upset. After all, ninety percent of the authority isn't bad, I'd say."

In practice, how much and what kind of authority should be delegated will obviously depend upon what needs to be done, who will be doing it, and other particulars of the situation. Neither Jack nor his boss are completely wrong. If Jack is to be held accountable for the success of the interviewing program, he needs an adequate supply of authority. Yet, in a hierarchical organization, a higher-level manager does have the right to approve every decision made by anyone in her area of authority; otherwise she could not be held accountable for how well her department functions.

Trouble starts when bosses and subordinates assume that the answers to "how much" and "what kind of" are equally obvious. And so they seem, until both blithely proceed with their own versions of how authority and responsibility were divided up. The result, as Jack and Jill discovered, is resentment and distrust. If you and your boss have such misunderstandings, your best bet is to negotiate a mutual agreement on the scope of your assignment and how much say you have in whatever decisions are part of that job.

For the best results, you'll need to engage your boss's interest without seeming so critical that you provoke an angry, placating, or guilty response. Avoid bringing up past disappointments. Accusations, veiled or obvious, intended or not, invariably evoke defensive reactions, quite the opposite of the "What's the problem and how do we fix it?" attitude that will result in workable agreements. Simply present your boss with a list of the tasks for which you believe you are responsible, stating the kind and amount of authority you believe you'll need to achieve your goals. An informal handwritten note seems to work best, probably because it seems less imposing. Be ready to make it clear that you're *not* trying to impose anything on anyone, that your sole interest is doing the best job possible. If your boss wonders why you are suddenly doing this, simply say, "I want to make sure we're in sync about what my job is and how much authority I have."

Start by thinking through how your position ought to relate to others, taking pains to choose the right words to accurately reflect the level of authority you believe you should have. Don't guess how your boss might describe your job or your authority level; don't anticipate how he will react to your proposals. On the other hand, be realistic—you're trying to initiate a useful discussion, not simply make a point or show your boss how inadequately he has been managing. For example, if it *is* your boss's job to set overall human-resource policies, *recommend* captures that appropriate level of authority that you ought to have for broad policy changes. In contrast, words like *set* or *establish* reflect the authority you should have over policies that pertain solely to staff members under your direct supervision. Don't restrict yourself to the formal aspects of how you and your boss will relate. For example, your delegation plan (for that is what you are in the process of developing) might properly specify that you will seek the director's consultation before you decide what the interview procedures will be. In proposing that, you're acknowledging that your boss has an interest in what you do, and a perspective different from yours, which you will want to consider when making your own decisions. Your statements might read something like this: "Consistent with human-resources department policies and after consultation with you, establish applicant interviewing policies and procedures."

Through it all, keep in mind that your purpose is a negotiated agreement with which you both can live. Encourage your boss to disagree with your view of your job, and where there are differences search for a middle ground. If you detect reluctance to go along with your authority to "establish policies," tuck in an "after consultation with you" to soften the blow. Remind him that delegating certain important decisions to you does not eliminate your boss's right to make those decisions final. With that in mind, you can commend her as a manager who has properly exercised that right by choosing to pass it on to you.

Breaking Through Behavior Blindness

Some people are remarkably obtuse about their effect on others, and especially how much their behavior bothers those who must put up with it. Such behaviorally blind people often have the best of intentions. They are no more out to hurt you than is a visually blind person who steps on your toe because she or he didn't know it was there. They rant, rage, bulldoze, or waffle at their friends, coworkers, and families, and then they cannot understand why others are so unhappy with them. None was more adept at not seeing how he affected others than Kirk Miller, who, when I first met him, had just been appointed the director of a major government agency. His list of managerial sins was of star quality. Not infrequently, I was informed by his subordinates, he publicly disparaged absent members of his staff, openly criticized them at public meetings, and had been heard to curse even junior staff who disappointed him. As disrupting as these behaviors were, none of them matched in sheer power to demoralize his habit of attaching derogatory notes, writ large, in bright red ink—"This is the stupidest thing I've ever seen"—to the top page of reports sent to him for review or approval, and then bouncing them back through the channels to the luckless originator. When I confronted him with these behaviors (his direct subordinates, political appointees all, it must be admitted, had been unwilling to face him), he was genuinely surprised, not by my descriptions of what he had done, but that others had reacted badly. "Sure, I lose my temper sometimes," he said, "but everyone around here knows that's just the way I am. Why, I've got a terrific staff here, all fine people, and they know what I think of them. Yeah, John Robbins (he was agency human-resources manager and a protected merit-system civil servant) had mentioned some of these things to me. He was a little fussed because of a few resignations, but I told him that anyone who is that sensitive is not going to be a good manager anyway. Don't you agree with me?" People like Kirk Miller are blessed—and cursed—with an internal filter system that screens out anything resembling negative feedback; thus they maintain their own comfort at the expense of others'. However, when and if—and it is at times a major *if*—you can break through that wonderful filter system, you can sometimes truly turn a wolf into a lamb.

Clearly, at that point, I had not yet penetrated Kirk's behavior blindness. Eventually, I did, by sticking pretty closely to the formula that follows.

Make an Appointment I believe you should always make an appointment with a boss to whom you are going to give potentially unpleasant feedback. Making a formal appointment communicates that you have something important to say. It also reduces the possibility that your discussion might be interrupted: by fellow workers who "only need a minute," by the telephone, or by secretaries with urgent papers to be signed. You can further emphasize importance and minimize interruptions by asking that all calls be held. Even if your request is refused for some reason— perhaps your boss may be expecting an emergency call from home—the request will demonstrate that you believe that you, and what you have to say, deserve to be taken seriously.

Talk About Any Ambiguities You Might Feel   Most people feel two ways about confrontational conversations, especially with their bosses. The need for the talk is great, but so is the apprehension. While you hope that your openness will reduce some rough edges in your relationship, you also know that there is no guarantee that your boss will not react with tears or anger. The best way to handle such an emotional bind is to talk about it. You might say something like: "To be honest, Mary, I've been feeling two ways about having this talk. On one hand, I think that it's really important and it will help our working together, but on the other hand, I'm not really sure how you are going to react to what I have to say." There are several reasons for starting off this way.

First, putting words to ambivalent feelings often relieves their intensity, decreasing the likelihood that you'll communicate your tension to your boss. While people who suffer from behavior blindness are quite well defended against direct accusations or complaining, they are often quite sensitive to unexpressed emotionality and when they dimly sense it, become even more defensive.

Second, after you have told your boss that what you have to say might produce an adverse reaction, you'll find it difficult to back out at the last minute. This "burning your bridges" technique can ensure that you'll proceed when your instincts are trying to propel you out the doorway.

Third, and most important, rarely can bosses—and I include very difficult ones—resist the impulse to show you that they can, indeed, react to your honesty with the attentive, calm attitude that is only to be expected from the mature, reasonable people they know themselves to be. In other words, you've set them up to listen responsibly to what you have to say.

Help Them Save Face People who feel denigrated seldom change productively, instead they become excessively defensive or abjectly self-blaming; neither state leading to much in the way of self-development. That is especially true when those whose behavior needs changing are largely unaware of just how much trouble they've been causing. Since your primary purpose in this undertaking is relief from your boss's nonproductive or aggravating behavior, the more you can reduce the accusatory nature of this interchange, the better. Try to stay focused on what needs to be changed, not on *who* is to blame, and, if at all possible, provide a ready-made excuse for any past sins, for example, your belief that your boss was unaware of how much you (and others) were bothered. Doing so will present you in a positive light, as a helpful friend rather than an accusing enemy. The general form of your statement might be: "The reason that I'm going into this, Boss, is because I'm sure that I haven't [or, I wonder whether we have] fully told you how much a few things that you do are interfering with my [our] work."

Describe the Difficult Behavior Having set the stage for candor and cushioned your boss's ego, you are ready to matter-of-factly set out both your boss's difficult behavior and the consequences to you, and to others, of that behavior. Keep in mind the twin rules for providing negative feedback: be specific and be descriptive. Psychologist Jack Gibb, who studied the conditions that promote defensive behavior, found that people became more self-protective when they were hit with generalized accusations—"You're always late"—than when the accusation was tied to specific incidents or kinds of behavior—"You were ten minutes late yesterday and today." Similarly, being labeled as a member of a tainted category—"Tom, you're a know-it-all"—raised defensive hackles more than a simple description—"Each time I make a point in staff meetings, you seem to re-explain everything I've said." Here are some examples of more specific and more descriptive statements:

"As the boss, you certainly have a right to choose your own work hours, Mrs. Smith, but I'm not sure you're aware of a problem I'm having when you come in as late as nine-thirty, I often find myself explaining to our clients why you're not available to answer their calls. They keep wanting to know when they should call in the morning to catch you in."

"When you talk to me about your disappointment in how John and Mary are working out, as you did both Tuesday and Friday, it interferes with my being able to work with them very enthusiastically."

It does take more time to be specific and descriptive than it does to be categorizing and general. However, by doing so, you'll increase the possibility that your points will be clearly heard.

Restate the Behavior-Blindness Assumption   As soon as you've offered the substance of your feedback, immediately restate whatever face-saving device you initially used. Something on the order of, "As I said, Boss, the reason that I'm going into all this is that I was pretty sure you didn't realize how much it was affecting me and interfering with our productivity."

Watch for Acknowledgment   If you are successful in breaking through, your reward will be the sight of a boss whose visage—whose entire demeanor—communicates shock, surprise, and even horror. While individual manifestations vary, a frozen face and posture, a changed complexion, and other signs of extreme tension are not uncommon. After all, the shock of seeing a part of yourself in a nondistorting mirror for the first time can unhinge anyone.

Provide Support   Having penetrated your boss's defensive wall, at least for the moment, you must now capitalize on it by providing support in as many different ways as you can. Since your goal was aiding a generally okay, if obtuse, boss to do less of whatever was the focus of your feedback, you'll need to make sure that the window of insight will remain open. Here are some ways to do that:

- Listen patiently to your boss's justifications. Show that you don't regard her as a villain by roughly paraphrasing what was said: "So, you talked with me about the other folks in the office because it helped you to think about how to handle them, is that correct?" "You were trying to solve one problem [Who can you talk to?] and inadvertently created another [my conflict of loyalties]."

- Acknowledge your boss's good intentions: "I can see that you were just trying to be a better manager."

- Indicate that you only expect him to "work on it," not become instant perfection.

- Make relevant suggestions: "Could you try to use the human-resources staff for advice on how to supervise Jim and Mary?"

- Indicate your willingness to provide feedback if and when unwanted behavior shows itself again: "Would it be a help if I were to mention it when I find I'm having to make excuses to clients again?"

Try a Dress Rehearsal Most people find providing honest feedback to a Difficult Boss singularly unappealing. As a way of lessening your apprehension, consider holding an abbreviated dress rehearsal of your part in the meeting, either by yourself, or, better, with a friend to take the role of your boss. Your friend will respond as your boss might (if your friend is not a coworker, you will have to briefly characterize your boss) or, if he simply hates to role-play, your friend can just sit there and look difficult. You, however, will be busy, trying out each step, doing and saying just what you will do and say with your boss. You'll act out setting up the appointment, especially if you expect to feel uneasy doing it, you'll ask that all calls be held, describe any ambivalence you'd feel, and so forth. After each step, ask your partner to comment on how you've done. In particular, ask about your approach. Were you matter-of-fact in tone—as opposed to accusing or nagging—but were you also direct—as opposed to indirect or hinting. Reprise any of the steps in which you faltered or in which you failed to maintain that calm, objective, positive mode for which you were striving. When you're satisfied you have the method in hand, reward yourself, then get on the phone and make that appointment.

Repairing Interaction Accidents

"How could I have ever deluded myself that Peggy Teller was a good boss," said Mike Wolfe to his wife one dreary Saturday morning, with more than a touch of self-pity. "The way she's been treating me the last few weeks has revealed the real Peggy Teller—a two-faced, egotistical tightass who's only out for herself. She cuts me down in staff meetings," he groused. "She scribbles smart remarks all over my advertising copy, and yesterday with everybody else around, she looked straight at me and started talking about maybe having to reduce marketing staff. But two can play at that game. If she wants to editorialize everything that I write anyway, there's no sense my busting my butt to make it first rate. Let her work every weekend rewriting my stuff, it serves her right."

"Aren't you just making it easy for her to ease you out?" asked his wife, Millie.

"Maybe so," retorted Mike as he reached for the employment section of the morning paper, "but that's okay with me. I don't want to work for that bitch a day longer than I have to."

Is Mike right? Is Peggy Teller a Jekyll and Hyde, once congenial and supportive, but now mean and vindictive? Possibly, but just as likely she was an essentially good person who, with Mike, was caught up in that universal human disaster, the Reciprocal Attack Spiraling Phenomenon, or RASP. To better understand how RASPs feed upon themselves, we'll need to revisit an almost trivial incident that took place one month before the bottom dropped out of what had seemed to Mike to be an ideal working situation. For six wonderful months he had blossomed as the junior member of the tiny marketing staff of a small but growing company. He had shown he could turn out readable copy; he was learning much about market survey, customer accounts, and how to make a product line more salable. Best of all, in Peggy he had found the perfect boss. She had a lively wit, she got on well with everyone, she went out of her way to help Mike over the rough spots, she even seemed to get a charge out of Mike's youthful enthusiasm. Then it happened: one unimportant, playful little remark tossed out at a staff meeting. Peggy was at the flip chart, lovingly laying out her ideas for a new ad campaign, when Mike, caught up in the intensity of an important planning session, butted in with, "Peggy, you are a very smart person, but that's really a dumb idea." Peggy barely blinked. Instead she smiled a little and said, "Maybe so," and moved on with her presentation. Mike continued to be active in the discussion, unaware that anything untoward had happened. The first signs of disaster hit him two days later. As he was walking into Peggy's office, her secretary had said sharply, "I'll let you know when Ms. Teller's free. If you have copy you can just leave it with me." "What's with the closed-door policy?" he quipped. "Is Peg on a status kick?" There was no reply.

Later, in the lunchroom, thinking that her secretary had merely been a little officious, Mike asked Peggy when he might see her. Peggy looked up without a smile and said, "Talk to Faye [her secretary] about when she can fit you in." Mike was now thoroughly confused. Doesn't she like my work? he wondered. To make sure that he hadn't somehow been slipping, he undertook his next two assignments with special care. Consequently he was stunned when they were returned just before the final deadline with a note that read, "Surely, you can do better." Two days later he came late to a staff meeting and openly stared at Peggy during the entire meeting. By the end of the week he was less surprised, but no less angry, to find that she had written her own copy for the two returned assignments, and, in addition, had informed him, also by note, that his new assignment was editing the employee newsletter, a task previously left for student interns. Mike's response was understandable, if not very constructive: He simply gave up trying to be productive and lapsed into the state we found him in as he perused the want ads two months later, on that gloomy Saturday morning.

To understand the spell by which bright, basically compatible people like Mike and Peggy can be transmuted into petulant children, let's further examine the anatomy of RASPs. In a sense, they are foreordained by the social nature of all human beings, because most of us wonder, and often worry, about how we appear to the people who are important to us. We search their faces, their behavior, their words, for clues. Do they appreciate how important, competent, likable, or powerful we are? What are their intentions toward us? When those clues, correctly interpreted or not, tell us that we have been ignored, dismissed, snubbed, shamed, or in any other way taken lightly, we retreat, attack, dissemble—sometimes all three. (Clever Peggy retreated and attacked with great economy by relegating Mike to her secretary's warm care.) Those on the receiving end of such unfriendly responses, often quite unaware of having trod on our psychic toes, naturally reciprocate with their own versions of cut-and-rip. We, in turn, see that uncivil behavior as evidence that our initial appraisal of evil intent was oh so true, and so the reciprocating attacks spiral ever downward. It is not surprising that the closer or more needful the relationship, the more sensitive the players are to the slightest clues that they are not fully loved, appreciated, or admired. The key point is that the provocation does not arise from what is said or done, but from the meaning and motivation ascribed to it. Poor Mike never intended his "That's dumb" remark as an insult. His "josh," as he later called it, was more a product of brash confidence, and two naïve presumptions: that Peggy's competence foretold an ironclad ego, and that her easy friendliness signaled an unconcern for the proprieties of organizational life. He was, unfortunately, wrong on both counts. Peggy had felt publicly ridiculed, and was furious that he, a neophyte whom she had "adopted," had questioned the soundness of her thinking. Unwisely, perhaps, she had shared her irritation at Mike with Faye, who dutifully pointed out that Mike—even though supposedly happily married—spent "too much time talking it up with the young secretaries." Further, Faye said, "some of the other staff question his sincerity." Sure, Peggy should have moved beyond her initially hurt feelings, called Mike in to let him know that she found his remark inappropriate, and checked out his intentions. It's simply good sense to make sure that your anger isn't being wasted on someone who was more mistaken than malevolent. But sensibleness is often the first casualty of hurt feelings, and Peggy reacted as most people do, with more vigor than thought. As did Mike. His assumption that the quality of his work was the cause of Peggy's ire led him to solve a reasonable but wrong problem. His carefully done pieces were interpreted by a wary Peggy as sly attempts to show off and once again show her up. Her only recourse, as all to whom she described Mike's behavior dutifully agreed, was to unequivocally show him who was boss. To an outside observer, unaware of Peggy's excellent relationships with others on her staff, she might seem a fair example of an intimidating boss. That same observer might wonder, as did Mike's friends at work—not to mention his wife—why he was acting like a surly brat. Yet a query to either of the principals would have placed the blame squarely on the other. It is this combination of perceptions that condemns to failure most naïve attempts to resolve these bitter feelings through straightforward dialogue. At times these attempts can even lead to an escalation of distrust. And once trust has been lost, it cannot be regained by avowals of trustworthiness, no matter how fervent or well meant. Fortunately such interactional disasters can be untangled, but to do so requires a knowledgable, step-by-step approach. But before we proceed with the cure, we need to address a prior question: How can you tell whether you are caught up in one of these confusing tangles or have simply encountered a difficult behavior type? What might lead you, in Mike's position, say, to suspect that Peggy's meanness might be the result of a RASP, rather than a manifestation of an Ogrelike personality?

Diagnosing RASPs

It's not always possible to differentiate the behavior of a Difficult Boss of the stripe we've seen in previous chapters from the RASPy end product of a relationship that has progressively soured. But if at least two of these indicators are evident, it's likely that interactional spiraling is involved: an abrupt change for the worse, a precipitating event, evidence that both parties have good relationships with others, and an awareness that even minor misdeeds infuriate you.

An Abrupt Change for the Worse   RASP-caused changes in behavior generally show themselves quickly—over a few days, weeks, or months—rather than as part of a slow deterioration. Since most people are to some extent moody, feeling better some days than others, it may not be immediately clear whether a sarcastic retort was due to a sleepless night or was the start of an interaction incident. Still, a relatively abrupt change in attitude should make you suspect that something you did has left your boss with a bruised ego.

A Precipitating Event   You'll have additional evidence that your boss's sudden slide into suspicion, coldness, or irritation might stem from a RASP if you can recall a recent event that might have left either of you feeling one down. Don't overlook incidents that, at the time, were dismissed as of little import, for full-blooming, perennial RASPs have often grown from trivial seeds. Some years ago I encountered a public health nurse and environmental sanitarian who, although they shared the same office, clientele, and car, had not spoken for over five years. The precipitating event was a note, left by the nurse for the sanitarian that read "Wash the car." She later recalled that she had intended to add a question mark, but, in a hurry, had neglected to do so. True, that note fell on fertile ground, since the two had never resolved the question of who was the senior person in their rural office (a horrifying example of crossed expectations). Nonetheless, that ambiguity had existed for two years prior to the incident of the infamous note, without an escalation. It was the sanitarian's response to the note, which was, one might say, in keeping with his trade, that provided just the fertilizer needed to ripen a budding RASP into a prize feud.

What makes the job of identifying such precipitating events difficult is the predilection of most people, while fully aware of their own sensitivities, to assume that others are—or ought to be—too mature to let minor slights bother them. "Don't sweat the little ones" is a wise enough maxim, but it doesn't square with the delicacy of most people's shaky self-regard.

So your task will be to try to recall what, if anything, went awry just prior to the disagreeable change in behavior. For example, you might remember that you did not include your boss in that informal staff pizza party you put together. Yes, it was because you were sure he would not want to come, and you suspected that, if he did, he might inhibit everyone else's fun. Even though you may have been right on both counts, it's also true, you now ruefully recollect, that he does like to be the center of attention, and he tries, albeit ineptly, to seem "one of the gang." In searching for an incident that may have started it all (an associate of mine calls them "interpersonal accidents"—I have visions of we poor human beings, careening through life, blithely denting each other's psychic fenders without looking back at the damage we've caused), bear in mind it's not what happened that counts, it's how it was interpreted by your boss that did the damage.

Relationships With Others Are Good   Since RASPs tend to bring out the worst in both you and your boss, but only in relation to each other, both of you will continue to have reasonable relationships with others. In checking this out, don't lost sight of the fact that when you complain about your boss to your coworkers, they may not directly contradict you. Be alert for blank looks, half smiles, slight nods or other evidence that they are simply trying to placate you. Your purpose is fact-finding, not gaining sympathy, so make it easy for them to tell you that, while they may not love your boss, they haven't encountered the array of difficult behaviors that are currently plaguing you.

The final criterion that will suggest that it's a RASP you need to repair is the level of your own emotionality.

Your Level of Emotionality Is Extreme   When your boss is smoldering at one end of a negatively spiraling interaction, you will be fuming at the other. You both will be seeing the other as a villain and letting go with whatever your own favorite difficult behaviors are. Therefore, if your stomach knots, your teeth grind, and you feel overwhelmed with helpless fury when you hear his or her footsteps echoing in the hallway, you are very likely ensnared in an interactional problem.

Now you are ready to take the steps that will help you to untangle a relationship gone awry.

Coping With RASPs

It was not long after his depressing Saturday that Mike—partly at his wife's urging—sought out Peggy to see if he could find out where he really stood. He waited until 5 P.M., the usual closing hour, and walked into her office where this "conversation" ensued.

Mike: Peggy, how could you simply reassign me to the employee crapletter without talking it over first?

Peggy: I don't have to talk to you about anything, but I can tell you that you're lucky you have any assignment at all.

Mike: Look, what did I do that was so wrong?

Peggy: (picking up her purse and briefcase): If you don't know, you're hopeless.

Mike: (mumbling to her back, as she walked down the hall): "Well, that's better than being a castrating bitch. Damn it! There is just no way to make an asshole like that be reasonable."

It's not an uncommon experience to try to patch up a spoiled relationship with an honest talk, only to find that you've worsened the situation you were hoping to improve. Words intended to clear the air lead instead to a recycling of old hurts and mutual recrimination. When trust is low, and hurts, real or fancied, are still keenly felt, it is not easy to calmly unravel emotional entanglements. This is especially true when the underlying causes were unintended, subtle, or forgotten slights, because most people are largely unaware of the magnifying power of negatively spiraling interactions. To break through the bitterness, a stronger medicine than "Let's talk this over" is needed. While conversation is still its basic ingredient, the how, when, and where of the following prescription will provide your best chance for regaining a healthy work relationship.

Step 1. *Make a Short-Fuse Appointment*

In the previous section on opening the eyes of a behaviorally blind boss, I suggested that a formal appointment readies your boss for a serious discussion and provides an easy first step into uncertain territory. Those advantages are equally pertinent here, with one proviso—keep the lead time short. To avoid adding fuel to an already smoldering emotional situation, try for an appointment with your boss as soon as possible after you ask for it; for instance, request a three o'clock meeting at two. You may be challenged about the necessity of the meeting; after all, at this stage your boss isn't feeling too kindly toward you, but try to avoid starting your discussion right there, that is, in the hallway or over the phone. "It's important, but I can't get into it until three," or "It's really too complicated to get into right now, but it is important," should get you out the door. Make as sure as you can that you ask for enough time to work your way through this relationship mess. Late afternoons, which allow the possibility of continuing after normal closing hours, are probably the best, even though you both may be tired. At minimum, make sure that you'll have at least an uninterrupted hour. Because the situation is already so fraught with emotion, try to avoid scheduling your conversation when either you or your boss are in the midst of a business or personal crisis.

Step 2. *Set the Stage*

As soon as you've entered your boss's office, ask that all calls be held so that you can "get the business done without interruption." I've been pleasantly surprised by the frequency with which even intimidating or angry bosses accede to that request when it is put forth matter-of-factly. If, however, your boss should refuse, don't make an issue of it. He or she may already be too suspicious of your intentions to be willing to cooperate at all.

Having seated yourself, alone and facing your hated (despised, feared, loathed) boss, and exquisitely wanting to get it all over with, you may be tempted to plunge straight into the roiling waters of confrontation. Instead, set the stage. Set a tone of civility by indicating that you appreciate your boss's willingness to meet with you. Check on the time limits under which you are operating, if that has not already been clarified. Most important, say a few words about what you hope will be the outcome of the meeting—the best possible working relationship. Try not to be seduced by a very understandable wish that *your* noble-sounding statement be met by an equally magnanimous gesture from your boss. That wish can turn into righteous resentment when, instead, you get nothing more than a cold stare. You avoid all that by *not* pausing after you've finished your stage-setting. (Note how RASPs continue to set up both parties for mutual disappointment.)

Step 3. *Comment on the State of Your Relationship*

Having set the stage, start off by commenting on the state of your relationship, as you've experienced it. Do your best to describe, rather than accuse, whine, or nag, give about equal time to your own problem behavior as well as that of your boss, and neither underplay nor overstate to make a point. End with your best guess (stated as such) of how you think your boss sees you. If you were Mike, you might sound something like this: "I'm not sure how you see it, Peggy, but I'm very dissatisfied with the way we've been working together. I feel like I've been letting down on my work, and turning things in that don't fit my own standards, and it seems to me that you've been taking some pretty critical potshots at me in staff meetings. I don't think it's my imagination that we haven't been as friendly as we were several months ago. My impression is that at this point you're pretty fed up with me. How does it look to you?"

(While it may seem a minor point, I'd suggest not ending with a question like "Do you agree?" For one thing, you can't be sure what is being agreed with. More important, you don't want to be sitting there staring at someone whose shouted, "You're damn right, I agree," is followed by silence.)

Step 4. *Prepare to Be Dumped On*

Having provided that sort of opening to someone who is thoroughly annoyed with you, what should you expect but a load of vituperation dumped right at your feet? It's vital that you begin this whole process of repair fully expecting to be vilified. Even then, you may find that your resolve to work things out is sorely tested. For it's common to be accused of horrible deeds of which you are guiltless, to have your motivations maligned, often in quite picturesque language, and to be told what a poor performer and/or person you are. Unfortunately, getting dumped on is a necessity for the successful completion of this coping approach. Not because "venting" anger dispels it, but because the first, and necessary, step in rebuilding trust is to reveal the suspicious and distorted perceptions so that they can be addressed.

Infrequently your boss's sole response will be a cold "Nothing's wrong." If your boss denies that there are problems in your relationship, you may be tempted to argue the point. That is usually unwise. Instead, express your pleasure that you were mistaken, and describe a rosy future relationship. "Wonderful, Peggy. That means we'll have lunch together as we used to, you'll give me face-to-face feedback on my work, and that some of the comments you've made about me were just your way of joking around. That being the case, you'll see a real turnaround in the kind of things I've been sending up to you." Having said that, be prepared for the "dumping" that you did not get before. If that does not occur, follow through on your assumption that your relationship has improved. If you find the door has remained shut, recycle back to Step 1. If you simply cannot break through, assume that you have a "Difficult Boss," review chapters 2 through 5, and start coping.

Step 5. *Convey Understanding Without Excuse or Apology*

After a thorough castigation, most people are hard put not to react defensively. Feeling guilty about their past performance, they may justify, or, pushed by their own escalating anger, they may riposte with equally acid comments. Regrettably, these very human responses don't help much. Thus the most demanding aspect of this step is not doing what comes naturally.

As a substitute for these natural, but not very constructive reactions, take pains to show that you did hear and understand what she said without agreeing or disagreeing with it. The best way to do this—it's often called "active listening"—is to roughly paraphrase back the essence of your boss's complaints about you, accompanied by a word or two to acknowledge the feelings that you surmise underlay those complaints.

You might sound something like this:

> "So, when I said what I did about your plan—saying it was stupid—you really felt undercut. It seemed like I was trying to show off in front of everyone at your expense. And the worst was that it came from someone you thought you'd treated really well."

Having demonstrated that you indeed got the message, without a pause, move on to the next step, describing your good intentions.

Step 6. *State Your Intentions*

Since the core of a RASP is a tangle of suspicious guesses that the other guy intended harm, it is the truth of those intentions that needs to be corrected if things are to get better. The essential ingredients of the correcting message are two phrases: 1) Certain events led you to think I meant to do you wrong; and 2) That was not what I wanted. For example, "Whatever I did in the past, my intention is to always be straight with you (do my best work, be a part of the team, etc.). Given the tension that is always part of these encounters, your boss may only hear that part of what you said that fits well with what he already believes—that you're a crumb. So be prepared for a reiteration of the negative things you've already heard. If that should happen, briefly recycle to Step 6, and once again, emphasize your own intentions.

If you can't avoid a discussion of past events, do avoid explaining your own behavior as a consequence of something your boss did—"When your secretary turned me away, I lost interest in doing good work." Instead, refocus on *your* impressions at the time—"When your secretary turned me away, I began to think that you were disappointed in the quality of my work." By emphasizing your *interpretation* of events, rather than the events themselves, you avoid setting in motion another frustrating round of counteraccusations, and, as a side benefit, you will have further "rehumanized" yourself in your boss's eyes.

Even if your efforts have been successful, you may not know it initially. For your boss will typically lean forward, stare at you for a few agonizing seconds, and then angrily snarl—"Well, that may be what you intend, Mike, but that sure as hell ain't what you've been doin'!" While the message may not be quite as explicit as this one, the key is a grudging acceptance that, as awful as your behavior was, your intentions may, in truth, have been benevolent. Your boss's original surmise about what was behind your behavior has now been opened to question, and you are ready for the final, but no less important, coping step, a move into the problem-solving mode.

Step 7. *Move to Problem Solving*

The magic of the problem-solving mode is that it focuses on the future. While problem solving draws on past happenings for data, its goal is to make things better from now on— your present purpose exactly.

Problem solving at this point serves two purposes. For one thing, it provides you both with something to talk about. You avoid the embarrassed silence or strained disengagement that might damage the fragile trust you've worked so hard for. But more important, it is the means for preventing future escalations. For example, you'll agree on a safety

mechanism for clearing the air early when future misunderstandings arise.

Problem solving need not be elaborate. An easy opening
phrase is, "What do we need to do to prevent this sort of
mix-up from happening again?" When Mike, having made
his way through each of the earlier steps, finally put this
question to Peggy, he was not sure how she would respond.
After her "That may be what you intend . . ." outburst, she
had turned her head toward the window and sat motionless
and withdrawn until he—unable to stand the silence—
asked the problem-solving question. Her response, however, made the wait worthwhile. "You've got talent, Michael (she had not called him Michael since their relationship began to erode), just use it. And," she added, "watch
your mouth."

"The first is easy," he said. "The second will take some
doing, but I'll work on it. Can I ask you to let me know if I
say anything that seems out of place to you? It may take me
awhile to learn when it's okay to shoot my mouth off and
when it isn't."

"Okay," said Peggy. "Why don't we talk about it some
more when we have our weekly one-on-ones."

"By the way," Mike said, as they were assembling themselves to go, "I'm sorry you had such a bad time over this."

"Well," said Peggy, "I guess I wasn't too easy on you."

While apologies made too soon can cut off full communication, after commitments have been made they can have a
rebuilding effect. However, the form of the apology should
be, "I regret that you were distressed," not "I'm sorry that I
was such a bad person." The first says only that you care,
the latter can seem like a request for forgiveness. Since
forgiveness often leaves both the forgiver and the forgiven
feeling one down, it adds confusion to a relationship just
when you're trying to keep things clear. Having been previously informed of that, of course, Mike merely smiled to
acknowledge Peggy's remark, putting down his impulse to
say, "Oh, that's all right."

8

Getting Into Action:
Plotting, Planning, and Protecting Yourself

Tillie shoved herself back from the cafeteria table and shot to her feet, barely aware of her chair crashing to the floor behind her. "That does it," she hissed, "I've showed you the letter we all signed; I tried to tell you how you've been screwing up with your staff; and all I get back is more bullshit."

"But Tillie," said Nancy, her section head, "I was only trying to explain . . ."

"Listen, you wimp," Tillie shouted, "there's no way you can explain to me why you didn't even send my promotion request up the chain. You can keep your free lunch and . . ."

"All right, Tillie, that's enough," shot back Nancy. "Maybe you'd better take a walk and cool down before things get out of hand!"

Tillie picked up her briefcase and looked around. Some of the late lunchers at neighboring tables hastily turned back to their plates. A few kept staring, with undisguised curiosity. Now I've done it, she thought as she walked out. All I wanted to do was tell Nancy that everyone in the section wanted her to be more supportive of us, and I've just royally screwed it up. Well, at least I got a reaction out of her, even if it was only to yell at me. But, now what am I going to tell the rest of the guys?

Poor Tillie. Too late she realized that while there are times and places for spontaneity and unrehearsed candor, a coping conversation with a Difficult Boss is seldom one of them.

Tillie's intention was on target—to give her boss, Nancy, direct feedback about some waffling behavior of which she seemed unaware. But Nancy's passively patient "explanation" seemed just another round of that same "listens, but never does anything to support us" attitude that had so irked Tillie and her coworkers. In retrospect it's not hard to see why her noble offer to bell the cat turned out badly. A few ill-chosen words, delivered accusingly in a noisy public place, were guaranteed to crank up Nancy's easily provoked defensiveness. In her enthusiasm—or perhaps it was her anxiety to get it over with—Tillie had moved ahead without a careful plan or thoughtful stage setting. The result—more setback than satisfaction. Always take the time to develop a coping strategy and plan before you tackle a Difficult Boss.

For one thing, there's your own tension level, it's likely to be high. The prospect of a possibly abrasive interchange can send your emotions into overdrive, a condition all too conducive to tears, tirades, and shooting from the hip. Knowing that you've worked out a handy map for finding the best path through unknown territory will lessen your apprehension and add to your confidence that you can cope with your boss effectively and safely. For example, a modicum of prior planning will help you to anticipate how your boss might react, preventing an unwanted sudden surprise, and equipping you with a fallback position, a way to cut your losses if the situation gets out of hand. Just what Tillie was not prepared for.

Equally important, a plan will avoid your applying the wrong technique to the wrong problem in the wrong way.

For example, without a plan you may find yourself confronting your boss at an inopportune time, in a place that is inimicable to intimate conversation. As Tillie discovered to her dismay, many people are distracted by the presence of others, even when little can be heard of what is said. Yet, while serious talk deserves a serious setting, not all coping conversations require grave tones and somber surroundings. There are times—when you need to demonstrate personal support for a waffling boss, for instance—when a breezy lunch may well be part of your approach. The point is that without reviewing what's happened in the past, setting reachable goals, selecting methods that fit your own style best, and carefully working out how you will bring up the bad news, you may not gain the positive results you wished for, and have a right to expect. A little plotting and planning is all that's needed to get it right.

The planning questions that follow are designed to help you to review what's happened in the past, set practical goals, identify other players who may hinder or help, select coping techniques that best fit you and your situation, and decide when and where to implement your action plan.

When you've answered them all, you may find that you've gained a more objective perspective, and that your initial skepticism about coping with your boss has given way to a cautious optimism that there might be at least some useful steps to be taken.

Planning Question 1:
What Does Your Boss Do That Bothers You?

What behavior has led you to characterize your boss as difficult? Be as specific and descriptive as possible. Pick some of the worst instances and describe just what your boss has done and said that you find objectionable.

Planing Question 2:
How Have You Both Reacted?

How have you reacted to your boss's difficult behavior? How did you feel? What did you say or do? How did your boss react to what you said and did? As much as you can, try for detail. Did you stand up? Did your boss point a finger? Did you look down? Specifics of that sort identify ways in which you may have unwittingly reinforced your boss's difficult behavior.

Planning Question 3:
What Kind of Difficult Boss Problem Is It?

Think broadly about your predicament, and probe for underlying causes that might not be apparent when your sole focus is on what hurts. Are there confusions about expectations and levels of authority, do you have a behavior blindness problem, have interactions gone sour? Do you simply have a boss who fits one or more of the specific difficult behavior types we covered in chapters 2 through 6? (Keep in mind that about 35 percent of the Difficult Bosses you might be unlucky enough to encounter bring at least two of those behavior patterns into play, although seldom both at the same time.)

It is possible, if unlikely, that all of the above underlying causes will apply to your boss. Don't give up. Instead, rank each one of them from most applicable to least applicable and plan to work from the top of your list.

Planning Question 4:
What Are Your Specific Goals?

The main question here is, what do I want my boss to do more of, less of, or do differently? Resist the temptation to wish your boss into a paragon of virtues. Reflect on what really hurts the most, or interferes the most with your own best performance. Do you value your boss's honest feedback, but wish that it would be delivered in a way that was less sarcastic, or in other ways demeaning? If you could count on your boss to actively support your next promotional opportunity, would that take the greatest edge from your having a boss who's otherwise not very strong?

You may find it helpful to start with a wish list of adjectives—*stronger, less hostile, less indecisive.* However, your final statement of your goals should also include the clues, subtle or obvious, that will tell you when those goals have been reached. Consider both what your boss does and how it affects you, related but not identical events. For example, if your boss has Fire-Eating tendencies, one indicator that you've made progress might be, *He will recognize when he's blown his cool and let me leave his office until he* *can cool off. Or, I will have a better notion of what sets my boss off and I will know how to soothe him before he blows up. Or, she may still blow her top now and again, but, if I understand what's happening, it won't bother me as much."**

Planning Question 5:
What Is Your Action Plan?

To this point you've assessed, as best you could, the nature and causes of your boss's difficult behavior. Your next step is to decide which actions offer the most chance for improvement. Review the portions of this book that seem most relevant to your own situation. Note what you will say to your boss, how you will try to say it, the most suitable timing and settings, and how you expect (not hope) your boss will initially react. Be as specific as you can. A general statement, such as "Tell my boss that he doesn't back me up," can leave you with only a hazy idea of how to broach the subject, a dry mouth and a vacant brain just when you most want to show yourself to best advantage. In general, the more tense you expect to be, the more your notes will resemble a film script, replete with stage directions.

Start small. Select a few moves that feel relatively comfortable and not very risky. Dipping a toe in the water before you take an icier plunge can be a confidence builder. Then, too, if you should fumble a little, the consequences won't be too great. For example, if your boss has Ogre-like tendencies, venture, "John, you interrupted me" when John has done so, but is otherwise in a mellow mood.

Give a thought to the times and places that will enhance whichever approaches you choose. For example, if you're

---

* I continually underestimate the healing that comes with a less personalized perspective of others' difficult behavior. When I ask clients "How did the coping go?" I find myself strangely frustrated when the response is a cheery "Fine. Now that I realize that Tom just has a short fuse, it's easy to shrug off his yelling and wait for him to get over it." No matter that they seem to really appreciate my help, my disappointment is there. I suppose that my unspoken cavil is "How could you let all those creative coping plans we worked on go to waste?"

going to attempt to untangle an interactional mess, try for a late-in-the-afternoon appointment so that you can continue past closing time, if necessary to ensure a long-enough pa- laver. The hours just before and after closing are also often the best times for securing uninterrupted privacy. Perhaps your boss tends toward moodiness. If so, plan to postpone any but the safest of coping steps until his mood cycles upward.

Planning Question 6:
What Other Players Need to Be Involved?

At times, your coping plan may need to include fellow workers, human-resources people, or your boss's boss.

Fellow Workers Grousing about Difficult Bosses with fellow employees is a common indoor sport, but it is not without its hazards. Angry complaining may seem like a harmless venting of supercharged emotions, but the consen- sus of most anger experts is that it is more likely to *increase* feelings of being put upon rather than alleviate them. In addition, griping can siphon off energy that would be better put to use in direct action.

There are, however, several good reasons to inform cer- tain of your coworkers about your plan. For one thing, you will be less distracted by concerns about how they might view your changed behavior. If they know why you're say- ing, "Ron, I disagree," they'll be less likely to panic, or, similarly, think you a sycophant when you flatter a Know- It-All supervisor.

Your coworkers may even want to join you, an advantage in several ways. Your confidence will grow and your fear of reprisal will lessen from the knowledge that others are act- ing with you. In addition, the greater the number of staff who do not feed your boss's difficult behavior with those habitual responses that make it so satisfying, the sooner that behavior will be dropped (or as learning psychologists phrase it, "extinguished").

Finally, if some of your coworkers might object to pro- posals you're planning, you'll want to know that in ad- vance, so you can modify them. For example, if you are trying to induce a Super-Delegator to hold more meetings, you'll need to ensure that the more hermitlike of your peers won't throw cold water on the idea.

Human-Resources Staff It's often wise to keep at least one human-resources contact informed of how you intend to deal with your boss. However, before you lay out your plan, make sure that what you say can and will be kept confidential. While many human-resources people do accept discretion as an important ingredient in building trust, some need to be reminded. It is also true that they are a part of management, and may be pulled by divided loyalties— wishing to be seen as a counseling resource to employees in need, but also feeling an obligation to keep senior management informed. Of course it may be part of your plan to use the human-resources staff as the safest and perhaps most effective way of informing higher levels of a situation that is affecting productivity or staff morale. If so, careful preparation is a must. A review of the sections in chapter 6 that pertain to whistleblowing might be wise before you decide on how to present your concerns.

Your Boss's Boss Put-upon employees have often told me that higher-level managers know just how obstreperous their subordinate manager—the troublesome boss—has become, and are ignoring, or even supporting, it. I've found that to be only partly so. Usually those senior managers are aware of, and disturbed by, the boss's behavior, but they do not know how to deal with it effectively. They may have tried, for example, by lecturing ("You've got to listen to your people more, Samantha") or by casually hinting ("You're doing a great job keeping up production, Charlie, but maybe you could communicate a little better with your staff"). Having "done all they could," they turn their attention elsewhere. Only further evidence that a serious problem exists will move them to try again.

Therefore, at some point you may decide to confer directly with your boss's boss. If you have previously established a reasonably good relationship, you may want to make contact soon after implementing your plan. Or, it may be a last resort because your boss isn't responding. In either case, here are some cautions and caveats.

Don't be surprised by an initially equivocal response from your boss's boss, a surface friendliness masking an incipient belief that you may be the problem person. Although you might receive wholehearted support from the start, I have, regretfully, found that a rarity. It's not that senior managers are uncaring about the mistreatment of employees. It's that you pose a painful dilemma—on one hand, an obligation to do something constructive, and on the other a likelihood that whatever it is, it will be time-consuming and disagreeable. By far the simplest—if less honorable—way for your boss's boss to resolve that dilemma is by hoping that you are the problem, a constant complainer, perhaps, or an incompetent getting revenge for a poor performance report. Thus, maddening as it may be to find yourself having to support the person from whom you expected support, it's to your advantage to avoid insisting that your boss's boss "do something."

In contrast, and this is an intriguing bit of business, you will both diminish resistance on their part, and gain powerful leverage by specifically asking that nothing be done until your own coping efforts have had a chance to take effect. This approach has two singular benefits, one obvious, the second perhaps less so. The obvious benefit is that you will show yourself to be an earnest, nontroublemaking employee, willing to solve your own problems and, incidentally, saving your boss's bosses from having to do something quite irksome. The second benefit stems from that curious human contrariness that Tom Sawyer made good use of in getting his friends to paint his aunt's fence by publicly allowing that he valued the task too much to let others share in it. In other words, don't be surprised if, having asked the big bosses not to intervene, your boss isn't taken into hand sooner than your jaded experience might have led you to believe.

In the same vein, do your best to avoid sounding like a chronic complainer. Your complaints may be justified, but the passive, even whining tone that sometimes accompanies complaining tends to elicit a placating or defensive response, neither of which will do much to enlist the assistance and support you need. Instead, stick with matter-of-fact, concrete descriptions of when and where your boss's harsh words were spoken, or what actions seemed unfair and vindictive. Extend your exposition far enough back to show that a pattern exists, but not so far back that your listener will become confused. Bring along notes, copies of caustic memos, and any other validating evidence you have. Of equal importance, be ready to document what you have already done to remedy the situation. For instance, you'll want to show how and when you brought the matter to the attention of your boss, what his reactions were, and whether any changed behavior resulted.

Even though you might resent having to do so—after all, you know you are not the problem—be ready to point out your own accomplishments. Bring along positive performance reviews, but don't depend upon them to show that you are indeed a satisfactory employee. Many managers are skeptical of laudatory reviews, having seen them misused to placate poor performers or pave the way for their transfer. Supplement your reviews with whatever other evidence of your value to the organization. Your objective is to show that 1) you are *not* the real villain and 2) you have evidence with which to prove it, should a more formal proceeding arise. A clue that you are indeed seen as the one to be dealt with, rather than the one to be helped, will be gentle subtle rebuttals, "It's funny, I haven't heard that before," or "Well, you know that John has been under a lot of pressure to get the work out lately." Forewarned, you will avoid an eerie sort of doubt about the reality of your own experience ("Maybe John really isn't so bad") and will keep yourself from channeling your frustration into an angry denunciation of your boss's boss ("You're all in this together").

Be Realistic About Your Goals   Sure, you'd prefer to see your inadequate, incompetent, or evil boss kicked out in disgrace, little enough to make up for what you've had to endure. But the firing or demotion of your boss is a goal best left until all of your other efforts have been unavailing. Start off your sentence with "What I would like" and focus on specific changes that would clearly enable you to be more personally effective in your job. Asking your boss's boss to get John to stop being abrasive, a label that can have many meanings, poses an impossible task and therefore will lead to inaction or to an injunction to John to "Treat your employees nicely, John, some of them are pretty unhappy." The Johns of the world are unlikely to be moved by such a plea. But, when you ask that John no longer insult you, shout at you when others are present, wax sarcastic when a simple statement will do, or give timely responses to your requests for promotion or a raise in pay, you provide senior management with behavioral changes that can be asked for and monitored. Even more important, almost everyone would agree that public scolding, harsh words, and lack of support for legitimate employee requests are signs of poor management. "Abrasiveness," on the other hand, has the ring of an immutable personality trait—not an area that most managers feel qualified to deal with.

Finally, to the extent that you can maintain a realistic tone, you will impress senior managers with your own maturity and dedication to the best functioning of the organization. That impression is potent. Nothing puts a manager's job at risk more than consistent clear allegations of ill treatment from employees who are seen as stable, mature contributors. And, if all else fails, you will be in an excellent position later on to say to your boss's boss, "John's behavior has not changed. Can we talk about what else might be done to remedy my problem?" It's always much easier to get a favorable transfer to another office, district, or boss when it is set in motion by a senior manager, than when you need to maneuver it yourself or, worse, gain the approval of the very boss you're trying to leave behind.

If your boss's boss openly admits a concern about your boss's behavior, but does not know how to proceed, try these suggestions, given in a "helpful hint" fashion:

- Ask the senior manager to set up a three-way conference—you, your boss, and your boss's boss—focused on how you and your boss can work together more effectively.

- Suggest that your boss might be less defensive if her boss brings up the difficult behavior as simply too much of a good thing: "We made you supervisor, Joan, because you're a strong go-get-'em person, but perhaps you're using too much of that great quality in dealing with your staff."
- Propose that your boss work with a management consultant who is knowledgeable about developing problem bosses. The human-resources department will often be able to make an appropriate referral.

Indicate That You Will Not Let the Matter Drop Bosses of difficult bosses, of course, always hope, albeit unrealistically, that they will never hear from you again. When you disabuse them of that hope you assist them in moving ahead with some corrective action even though they are sure—and usually quite rightly—that it will be unpleasant. Offering to let them know how things are going in a month or so will usually suffice. Your request for a follow-up meeting should not be a threat but merely a proposed conference between two people who are both interested in solving the same problem. Remind them that a follow-up meeting with you will serve a valuable purpose. Without a mechanism for checking on how well their attempts at ameliorating the problem have fared, it's quite understandable that they may wrongly assume that whatever they did was sufficient. Try to get across the point that providing you with a safety valve will help you remain more objective about the whole thing, and reduce the possibility of a public explosion, a hasty grievance, or legal action.

Decide ahead of time whether you want to ask that your conversation with your boss's boss remain confidential. Your reasons for asking that your boss not be told might be fear of reprisal or simply a wish to avoid an unpleasant confrontation. Nonetheless, regardless of what is promised, your name may be mentioned anyway. While your boss's boss may *intend* to leave you out of future discussions, he orshe may slip, or be badgered by your boss into giving your name.

Consider how you will react if that should happen and

your boss confronts you. The best initial response may be a straightforward, "I tried to talk to you about it but you didn't seem to listen." Follow this with a suggestion that you both meet with your boss's boss to work out a plan. If your boss takes an aggressive tone and accuses you of deserving whatever treatment you've received, do your best to maintain your own matter-of-fact problem-solving attitude. You might say, "Sally, can we leave this all in the past? Tell me specifically what you expect from me and what standards you'll use to judge me against. I'll do my best to meet them. In return, I'll expect that you will treat me with courtesy. For example, you will do your best not to be sarcastic when I've made a mistake." If it's obvious that you will be meeting again with your boss's boss, commit yourself to report any improvements in your relationship. Avoid the implication that you are now the evaluator of your boss. It will sound demeaning—after all, he or she is your superior and you're not supposed to be the judge. Instead, stay with problem-solving language, for example, "It's what will happen from now on that I'm interested in and I'll certainly tell Mrs. Jones about changes in the way we're working together."

Planning Question 7:
How Will You Monitor Your Plan?

The most ubiquitous characteristic of plans is that they usually need changing. When the subject is people, the key word is *always*. So keeping an eye on how well your plan is working is essential. To monitor your plan you'll need to find answers to questions like these:

- Am I actually doing what my plan called for?
- Did I, perhaps, peg my boss as the wrong difficult type, confusing a constantly bullying Ogre with a Fire-Eating monster who only attacks when I overrun a deadline?
- Can I see any results? What seems to be working well? What is not?
- How should I modify my approach, given my boss's reactions to my first efforts?

- How am I doing personally? Am I feeling more or less powerless to deal with this situation?
- Would my obtaining counseling or training—on how to communicate more assertively, say—be helpful?

In addition to their value in reshaping your plans, updating your answers to questions like these will help you stay objective and buttress your sense of being an active coper, rather than a passive victim.

When your coping begins to pay off—your boss actually supports your request for a raise, a promotion, or expanded duties—you may feel justifiably elated and relieved that it's all over. Nonetheless, it is usually unwise to relax your efforts at that point. While some improvements are self-maintaining, others will have resulted primarily from the steps you've taken. If you cut back too soon, the same inner forces that produced the difficult behavior in the first place may do so once again. You can mitigate this backsliding tendency by periodically hauling out your tried-and-true coping techniques ("Ron, you interrupted me"), and by complimenting your boss on her or his part in the improved relationships ("You're still one tough dude, Ron, but, since we started having two-way conversations you're more fun to work for").

Review Your Plan With a Friendly Counselor

It is often helpful to talk over your plan with a friend or counselor. At a minimum you'll gain perspective as you hear yourself outlining your projected course of action.

At best you may find someone who is willing to act as a coach, raising questions, suggesting embellishments or cautions, and even providing a live target on whom you can try out your initial coping statements. Is your first bite too large? Do your scripted coping comments smack more of angry denunciation than matter-of-fact feedback? Or, are they so indirect that they will only serve to make your too timid boss anxious rather than assertive?

Professional counselors can serve these purposes admirably, especially if they have had organizational experience of their own. Without that "street knowledge" of the boss-subordinate relationships, a well-intentioned counselor may try to refocus you from how to cope with your boss to why she or he bothers you so much. While that is a legitimate counseling issue, it is not a substitute for taking action to directly minimize your boss's troublesome behavior.

Personal friends can also be helpful coaches, if they will be candid, and if they won't simply agree with you that your boss is awful, and then regale you with war stories of their own. While "all bosses are rats" conversations can be sources of amusement and momentary relief, they do not help you to get on with the task of developing a well-worked-out coping plan.

Coping With Difficult Bosses Is a Great Idea, but It Isn't Easy

If you are like most people, you will view dealing directly with your boss's difficult behavior with an ambivalence that verges on outright trepidation. You *do* want to feel more productive or less stressed, but you aren't at all sure that you want those benefits enough to court whatever risky business may turn up along the way. At the heart of that reluctance to get started—and you have lots of company—is usually one of these three most frequently cited concerns: fear of making things worse, a nagging worry that you might be the difficult one, and a sneaky little rationalization that the trouble it takes isn't really justified because your boss is not the worst in the world. Not surprisingly, the best way to surmount these final guardians of the status quo is to acknowledge them, and by so doing, reduce them to manageable size. Here are some thoughts about the sense, and nonsense, in each of them.

Fear of Making Things Worse

Bosses certainly have the power to make your work life worse. They can withhold raises, favor others with the interesting jobs, assign you to the disagreeable tasks, allow your promotions to wither on the vine, and in a hundred like ways harass you. Given these realities, it's not surprising that many are tempted to live with a boss's difficult behavior rather than risk a vindictive counterattack. Yet, my experience is that knowledgeable efforts at coping with a Difficult Boss rarely lead to negative consequences. I believe there are several reasons for this.

Their Power Is Limited For one thing, most people attribute considerably more power and authority to their bosses than even the bosses believe they have. With the exception of owner-managed small businesses, hiring, firing, and salary decisions are seldom made without overview from more senior managers and human-resources staff. While bosses with Ogre-like tendencies do sometimes react to challenges to their authority with vigorous, aggressive moves of their own, their ability to fire or demote an employee who has done nothing more than stand up to them is severely limited. "I want to let her go because she objected to my insulting her," is not likely to find much support. True, there are devious ways to punish, too often used by devious people, and when you are faced with this possibility, it is especially wise to start small, carefully plan your moves, and continually test the coping waters as you proceed. As an added measure of safety, you may also need to buttress your coping campaign with the kind of documentation I suggested in chapter 6 and earlier in this chapter, so that, if need be, you can avail yourself of whatever organizational and legal remedies are available.

Coping Techniques Don't Provoke In addition, the coping techniques themselves have proven effective because they reduce the impact of difficult behavior in a nonprovocative way, a useful fact to remind yourself of when you're feeling apprehensive.

The Worst-Case Analysis Finally it's always useful to buttress yourself against a fear of unpleasant reprisals by beginning with that gloomiest of undertakings (pun intended), the worst-case analysis. It is a reliable technique for gaining perspective by rehearsing a series of pessimistic scenarios. The process is simple. Suppose, for example, that you have decided to try the "Ron, I disagree with you, but tell me more" technique on an intimidating boss. You'll start your worst-case analysis by asking yourself What is the worst that can happen? Ron might be furious and I'll get yelled at, may be a reasonable guess at his reaction. And then what would I do? you'll ask yourself. I'd probably be petrified and just stand there. And then what would happen? He would eventually get tired of yelling if I didn't provoke him, and I'd be no worse off than I was before, might be your conclusion. Almost invariably, when I have walked my clients through such a sequence of unhappy consequences, they have found them not as fearsome as they had imagined. That is even the case when, based upon their own experience, or that of others who were indeed badly treated, they faced the worst—Ron would fire me. In keeping with the method of worst-case analysis, I would ask, "And then what would happen?" Often the answer was, "I'd heave a sigh of relief and get another job." They were then ready to begin coping. Sometimes the circumstances of their lives made finding another job seem impossible. Even then, room to maneuver might be found, for example, by differentiating between *impossible* and *costly*. A move that necessitates a reduction in rank or pay may yet be a favored alternative if the boss's antics are leading to continuous anger or depression, and consequently to ill health.

What If I'm Difficult Too?

If you are like every other living human, you have occasionally been told by friends, coworkers, or family members that you are at times irritating, exasperating, or hard to understand. And in your more introspective moments you may even agree that you are sometimes at least a little difficult. While such candor about your personal fallibility is laudable, the acknowledgment of your own hot temper does not transmute your boss's tantrums into acceptable behavior. For one thing it's their *job* to help you perform optimally. Even more to the point, the power and authority that accompanies their designation as managers imposes, or should, a special responsibility to use that power and authority fairly and with restraint. I'm not proposing that you are not responsible for your own self-development, nor ignoring the possibility that you may inadvertently be bringing out the worst in your boss. By all means admit that you can be a bit difficult; it is a commendable first step toward managing your own troublesome behavior. Rather, I'm suggesting that, whether or not you need to attend to your own development, you have a right to do what you can to minimize your boss's difficult behavior.

Is It Worth the Effort?

At times the attention and effort required for coping effectively may tempt you to grudgingly accept your boss's behavior because "he's not always all that bad." After all, so your reasoning might go, everyone has some weaknesses, and I've heard of bosses who were a lot worse than mine. Do I really want to go to all that trouble to improve a situation that isn't so horrible? Certainly all difficult bosses are not equally bothersome. For example, some intimidators only browbeat sporadically; they are awful when on the warpath but bearable when not. From that perspective, it may seem sensible to soft-pedal serious coping efforts, conserving your strength for other battles in other places. As one of my clients succinctly put it, "Dr. Bramson, you're giving me an extra job on top of the one I've already got—who needs it?" However, before you decide that your boss is not bad enough to bother with, I suggest that you consider the following criteria. I believe they describe the minimum that any employee ought to be able to take for granted from a boss. Bosses who are *not* difficult will:

- treat you with courtesy and avoid sarcastic or insulting remarks.
- manage as they say they intend to manage. For

example, when they say "I value your input and will ask for it before I make a decision," they will usually seek your input before important decisions are finalized. (Keep in mind that *seek* is not the same as *follow*. Your boss may have legitimate reasons for not taking your advice.)

• use their power to achieve organizational goals rather than to feather their own nests. (This doesn't mean that they might not personally benefit from attaining organizational goals.)

• represent the needs and wishes of those who report to them to higher levels, even when it requires moderate risk on their part.

To the extent your boss does not live up to these reasonable expectations, I believe you have a right, perhaps even a responsibility to yourself, to take an active coping role. The best course for you may depend less on how difficult your boss is than on the personal importance of your job. If your work is a major underpinning of your self-esteem, you can't afford to let an even moderately bad boss erode it.

On the positive side, bosses who are only moderately difficult are usually the easiest and least scary to cope with.

What If It Doesn't Work?

Suppose your best coping efforts seem unavailing. The bullying continues, your Artful Dodgers still leave you in the lurch, your best decisions are invariably second guessed and your boss's boss is unable, or unwilling, to help. What then? There are no hard and fast answers to this question. However, you'll need to consider these points before you decide:

• Have your efforts to cope effectively with your troublesome boss been as persistant, planned, and skillful as you believe they can be?

• Is it worth so much energy and attention?

• How hard would it be for you to get some distance

from this person short of quitting your job? For example, can you apply for a transfer to another unit or another region? Would a demotion be a worthwhile price for a less distressing work situation?

- What are the costs to you if you continue to work for a manager whose behavior distresses you? Chief among the costs you should assess is the degree to which you experience that killing combination of frustration, anger, and helplessness. If prolonged, it can have serious consequences to your health.
- How favorable is the current job market? Are enough suitable jobs available in your area to make escape a better alternative than continued efforts to cope?

I have led more than a few thoroughly exasperated clients through these questions of last resort and have often been struck by a curious turn of events. They had endured much from their impossible bosses, they were tired of trying to cope, and, as one or two admitted—they were fed up with my smug suggestions about how to do it better. There was, they believed, nothing left but to get away from both of us. With that choice behind them, and thus with little to lose, they would then return to their coping chores with just enough dash and confidence to make them work. Their Difficult Bosses became at least bearable—in some cases even admirable—and my clients' sense of self-efficacy leaped high.

Coping with a Difficult Boss is never restful in contemplation, and it can have its anxious moments in execution. Yet, all that I've seen leads me to believe there is good cause for optimism. For most of the Difficult Bosses that comprise the collection of cases in this book were changed for the better by the coping efforts of their sometimes desperate subordinates. What they did, you can do, too.

Bibliography

Bandura, A. *Social Foundations of Thought and Action.* Englewood Cliffs, N.J.: Prentice Hall, 1986.

Bramson, Robert. *Coping With Difficult People.* New York: Doubleday, 1981.

Bramson, Robert. *Coping With the Fast Track Blues.* New York: Doubleday, 1990.

Burley-Allen, Madelyn. *Managing Assertively: How to Improve Your People Skills.* New York: John Wiley and Sons, 1983.

Ellis, Albert. *A Guide To Rational Living.* Hollywood, Cal.: Wilshire Books, 1975.

Fisher, R., and W. Ury. *Getting to Yes.* Boston: Houghton Mifflin, 1981.

Fromm, Erich. *Man for Himself.* New York: Fawcett Publications, 1947.

Frost, P., V. Mitchell, and W. Nord. *Organizational Reality Reports from the Firing Line.* 3rd ed. Glenview, Ill: Scott Foresman, 1986.

Grothe, M., and P. Wylie. *Problem Bosses: Who They Are and How to Deal with Them.* New York: Berkely Books, 1982.

Harrison, A., and R. Bramson. *The Art of Thinking.* New York: Berkely Books, 1982.

Kelly, George. *The Psychology of Personal Constructs.* New York: W. W. Norton, 1955.

Kets de Vries, Manfred, and Danny Miller. *The Neurotic Organization.* San Francisco: Jossey-Bass, 1984.

Lombardo, Michael and Margan McCall. "Coping With an Intolerable Boss," *Center for Creative Leadership Special Report.* January 1984.

McDonald, D. "How to Tell Your Boss He Is Wrong", *Management Solutions,* December 1988.

Monat, Allen, and Richard Lazarus, eds. *Stress and Coping.* New York: Columbia University Press, 1985.

Morrisey, George. *Getting Your Act Together.* New York: John Wiley and Sons, 1980.

Plas, Jeanne, and Kathleen Hoover-Dempsey. *Working Up a Storm.* New York: W. W. Norton, 1988.

Schaef, Anne. *Co-Dependence Misunderstood—Mistreated.* New York: Harper and Row, 1986.

Schaef, Anne, and Diane Fasel. *The Addictive Organization.* San Francisco: Harper and Row, 1988.

Sethi, A., and R. Schuler, eds. *Handbook of Organizational Stress Coping Strategies.* Cambridge, Mass. Ballinger, 1984.

Tavris, C. *Anger: The Misunderstood Emotion.* New York: Simon and Schuster, 1984.

Weisinger, H. *The Critical Edge.* New York: Little Brown, 1989.